WHAT DO YOU DO NOW?

ETHICAL ISSUES ENCOUNTERED BY CHARTERED ACCOUNTANTS

by

Dr David Molyneaux
Aberdeen University

Published by

The Institute of Chartered Accountants of Scotland
CA House, 21 Haymarket Yards
Edinburgh EH12 5BH

First Published 2008
The Institute of Chartered Accountants of Scotland

ISBN 978-1 904574-47-7
EAN 9781904574477

This book is published for the Research Committee of The Institute of Chartered Accountants of Scotland. The views expressed in this report are those of the author and do not necessarily represent the views of the Council of the Institute or the Research Committee.

Printed and bound in Great Britain
by T. J. International Ltd.

CONTENTS

Foreword .... *i*
Acknowledgements .... *iii*
Executive Summary .... *v*

1. INTRODUCTION 1

Rationale and context 1
Legal considerations 5
The historical vision of ethics for accountants 7

2. THE METHODOLOGIES OF RESEARCH AND ANALYSIS 9

Introduction 9
Methods of research 9
The research's limitations and potential, and use of the term 'scenario' 12
Methods of analysis 15
The tentative nature of the analysis 18

3. THE 'GUARDIAN' AND 'COMMERCIAL' ETHICAL SYNDROMES .. 19

Introducing the concept 19
Different roles and different interpretations of ethical values 21
Implications of distinguishing the functions 22
Significance of the risks and opportunities of accountancy ethics .. 25

4. The Case Study Scenarios 29

Using the scenarios 29
Brief summaries of each scenario's context, level and principal ethical issues 31
The scenarios 34

5. Conclusions 193

The essential, but unstated, principle, of 'ethical courage' 193
Loneliness, agencies for professional support and the ethical essentials of 'conscience' and 'self-discipline' 197
Reflections on the 'Guardian' and 'Commercial' theme and the ethical principle of 'discernment' 199
Wider reflections and the prospective role of accountants for the promotion of professional ethics 201

References 205

FOREWORD

Ethics and integrity lie at the heart of the qualities expected of Chartered Accountants. The Institute of Chartered Accountants of Scotland (ICAS) has commissioned and published a number of important works in this area over the past few years. This research report looks at ethical challenges in a new and refreshing way.

How often do we ask ourselves "what should I do?". This report collates twenty eight true-life ethical scenarios faced by accountants either in practice or business. The objective of the report is to bring ethical problems to life and to encourage debate and understanding of such issues rather than providing definitive answers. Each scenario concludes with "What do you do now?", before identifying factors to be considered, and offering analysis of these.

The scenarios are a reminder of how real dilemmas can either emerge over time or present themselves without warning. The scenarios provide resources for accountants that can be used in many ways. They can be discussed informally with colleagues to assess what each might do in these circumstances. They can be used for more formal training and educational purposes and, perhaps, in other novel ways to ensure that ethical challenges are debated and properly understood within the profession, in practice and in business, and in academia.

This project was funded by the Scottish Accountancy Trust for Education and Research (SATER). The Research Committee of ICAS has also been happy to support this project. The Committee recognises that the views expressed do not necessarily represent those of ICAS itself, but hopes that the project will encourage debate on ethics within the profession and academia.

David Spence
Convener, Research Committee
April 2008

ACKNOWLEDGEMENTS

By the nature of this report, those who contributed to it most, by providing directly the core confidential material for the scenarios, must remain anonymous. Nevertheless their support has been foundational. Many other Chartered Accountants and members of staff at ICAS have assisted indirectly with insights as it progressed. The academic and practitioner reviewers gave valuable suggestions as it neared completion.

Christine Helliar as Director of Research and Michelle Crickett as Assistant Director of Research at ICAS have provided cheerful encouragement and enduring patience to maintain the momentum amid many distractions.

Angie Wilkie of ICAS has dealt expertly with the unusually complex demands of dealing with the unusual layout of the report and George Molyneaux has helped with reviewing the text.

Bill Hutton has been a tireless friend, a stimulating correspondent and a source of much wisdom on ethical conduct in all aspects of business and professional life. Moreover, he has demonstrated how ethical courage and determination are essential if ethical values are to be sustained and respected in practice - the real proving ground of any principles and theories.

Finally, the Research Committee and the researchers are grateful for the financial support of the Trustees of the Scottish Accountancy Trust for Education and Research, without which the research would not have been possible.

EXECUTIVE SUMMARY

This report records a series of 28 experiences of ethical challenge that have been faced by Chartered Accountants (CAs). The circumstances of each are set out in a scenario that ends with the question: '*What do you do now?*' It is hoped that this format will help readers derive an increased sense of the acuteness of the issues and the pain of making decisions where there is an ethical dimension. The overall objective is for readers to encounter the ethical problems as directly as possible rather than, say, look to receive remedies prescribed for some anonymous other person by some anonymous committee.

Nature of the study

As outlined in chapter one, using short case-studies, or parables, is an ancient presentational method to stimulate consideration of ethical issues and appropriate responses by individuals. Traditionally, such stories have helped to maintain focus on an enduring and compelling need. Ultimately, any exploration of ethics is for the purpose of finding pragmatic solutions to real-life problems. Termed a 'scenario' in this report, each one in the series is a resource that is now available for accountants at any stage within their careers: to be reflected upon, to be compared with their own experiences and to be discussed with colleagues (preferably both senior and junior) in order to develop a clearer personal understanding of the nature of ethical professional conduct.

Yet, while there is an educational function for this report, it is not a training manual. For example, it does not stipulate the detailed application of certain formal regulations within the UK whereby, for example, confidentiality should be breached to comply with regulatory requirements. To engage comprehensively with such clauses might risk confusing broad ethical expectations with current legal obligations, and, indeed, only the obligations found in one jurisdiction. Rather, the report is intended to encourage thinking about wider aspects of 'being an accountant' and it cannot substitute for the necessary but separate task of familiarisation with statutorily-defined duties.

Sourcing the study

As explained in chapter two, in order to prompt meaningful debate over appropriate actions, scenarios on ethical issues must be relevant and credible. To reflect reality they must include sufficient complexity and nuances to allow for diverse possibilities. The sourcing of the scenarios in this report has been through confidential interviews with volunteer CAs drawn from different backgrounds and specialisations within professional practice and industry. To respect their entitlement to confidentiality, the circumstances of their stories have been amended so that, while key points remain valid, individuals and clients are untraceable.

Analysing the scenarios

To assist readers in identifying the possible significance of ethical features of the scenarios, an analysis has been prepared for each, addressing the common questions of:

1. What are the readily-identifiable ethical issues for your decision (distinguishing where relevant between the individual accountant and the professional firm)?
2. Who are the key parties (including 'you') who can influence, or will be affected by, your decision?
3. What fundamental ethical principles for accountants are most applicable and is there an apparent conflict between them?

4. Is there any further information (including legal obligations) or discussion that might be relevant?
5. Is there a conflict between the 'Guardian' and 'Commercial' strands of an accountant's responsibilities?
6. Based on the information available, is there scope for an imaginative solution?
7. Are there any other comments?

These questions may be changed or supplemented by each reader's own questions, for these analyses do not purport to be model answers. To do so would seem both to claim an unwarranted authority and to be self-defeating to the aims of the whole project. Suggesting that any single, apparently-definitive 'right' answer actually exists could kill off discussion. Rather, the purpose of collecting and publishing the research is to promote critical thinking and wider discourse so that individuals and groups can tease out for themselves what they think they ought to do in such situations. In reality, a discerning accountant may be forced to recognise that ambiguity, rather than a hoped-for simplistic perfection, is inevitable. The goal is then to find a principled yet pragmatic solution that will fit best to the unique circumstances of each ethical challenge. Respecting principles, rather than adhering to rules, means advance preparation through exploring processes and seeking self-understanding, rather than expecting to receive prescriptive answers.

'Guardian' and 'Commercial' perceptions of ethical issues

To help this self-understanding, within each analysis is an innovative approach to examining the dual nature of many an accountant's role. The need for judgement to determine what constitutes 'true and fair' in financial reporting requires a combination of skills and talents, particularly for an auditor who is directly at the cusp between 'Guardian' and 'Commercial' functions. As chapter three describes, within any society, 'Guardians', such as judges, the police or the military, establish and protect a secure framework within which 'Commercial' traders, manufacturers and service industries can prosper. These twin foundational purposes will foster distinct values and stimulate separate cultures responsive to the needs of the respective practices. While some ethical expectations will be shared, prioritisations will differ. While 'Guardians' may prize respect for precedents, organisational loyalty and steadfast determination, those in 'Commerce' will emphasise inventiveness, thrift and openness to strangers. Auditors, acting as 'Guardians', are required to deliver a formal, quasi-judicial opinion while simultaneously seeking to sustain or create new relationships with 'Commercial' clients through a knowledgeable familiarity with the dynamics of their businesses. Auditors, as with accountants in many roles, must also negotiate over fees, timetables, wordings of reports and related matters in a manner that would, rightly, be an anathema to judges.

Because financial reporting is intrinsic to almost every conceivable collective activity, all accountants seeking to adhere to the demands of 'true and fair', whether or not acting as auditors, are likely to encounter contrasting, sometimes conflicting, ethical outlooks from various other professions. In this report, it is hoped that by highlighting the existence and potential tensions of these two foundations, accountants may more readily recognise the systemic ethical risks of the different yet combined modes in which they must operate. Thus, they can explore how a spirit of 'heroic' independence - of integrity, objectivity and public service - may best be demonstrated within the established frameworks through which they deliver their professional services.

The scenarios

Chapter four focuses on the scenarios themselves, having first indicated the contexts and ethical concerns of each. Every narrative stands alone but, for ease of reference, twenty have been grouped loosely under headings to show the setting and accountancy activity in which the 'you' of the scenario is currently working. These cover, 'Professional firm/general practice', 'Family business', 'Audit', 'Audit with tax complications', 'Tax practice', 'Consultancy services' and 'Insolvency'. The remaining eight are grouped under the headings of 'Public interest', 'Non-profit and recruitment' and 'Professional relationships' to indicate the more generic nature of the circumstances described. This allocation is relatively arbitrary but the disparity reflects the facts of what volunteers selected to reveal and what they decided had an ethical dimension.

For each scenario, an indication is given of the career level of the 'you' but this definitely need not be the same situation as that of the reader. Rather, the scenarios offer a useful opportunity to explore the experiences and ethical challenges of accountants in positions other than the reader's own. Specialist technical knowledge (beyond that briefly explained) should not be necessary. In the index there is a very short summary of the principal ethical issues found in each scenario but, as with the analyses, the reader may identify others.

Conclusions

Chapter five offers less by way of 'conclusions' than might be expected of a more conventional report. Throughout, readers have been invited to determine their own reactions and the wider implications from the researched material. Thus, chapter five points to aspects of the exploration that may have been less explicit in the preceding chapters. These include a brief review of the underlying need for 'ethical courage', whether instinctively to counter fears or to prevent the excessive exploitation of professional privilege. Whilst scenarios can simulate the weighing up of responsibilities, they cannot point precisely where, within the personal spectrum between timidity and temerity, each individual might actually need to act. Yet, it seems essential to note that without 'ethical courage', assertions about fundamental ethical principles may prove to be of little more substance than platitudes with a veneer of piety, or outright hypocrisy.

Another, allied, theme that emerged from the research is that of the sense of loneliness for many individuals when faced with the pain of decision-making. From this flows the importance of seeking external supports, such as from the counsellors and advisors employed for this purpose by professional institutes, and of using internal supports, such as corporate or professional 'conscience'. While 'freedom of conscience' is an individual human right, the setting and maintaining of collective corporate or professional conscience requires clear and constructive communication. It is beyond the scope of the report to do more than signal its fundamental significance, as too with 'self-discipline'. An accountant's training that promotes 'balance' and 'reconciliation' should set boundaries, encourage self-control and help develop a concern for principled compromise in implementation. The scenarios and related analyses are intended to be a contribution towards creating a language for collective conscience but they will be of limited practical benefit if necessary self-restraint is not also applied.

Chapter five also revisits the distinctions between the 'Guardian' and 'Commercial' roles and their symbiosis in aspects of the accountant's art. It suggests that the ethical attribute of 'discernment', or practical wisdom, is essential to manage the inherent contradictions to generate a healthy and creative tension. By building on technical competence and diligence, a discerning accountant can ensure that both integrity and objectivity are most effectively deployed for the mutual benefits of public, client and personal interests alike. Powers of discernment may come through training, reflection and imagination and may also be utilised in mentoring and dispute resolution. Hopefully, the scenarios and the analyses can form part of the processes for enhancing discernment within the community of professional accountants.

The report ends by noting how the pivotal and privileged position of the accountancy profession leaves it well placed to provide leadership to society. However, members must first determine whether they want consciously to set out to promote higher standards of ethical expectation and moral leadership to the society in which they live, or whether it is acceptable only to adopt and adapt to the norms of contemporary 'best practice', while being under no obligation to try for its extension. For this, the report acknowledges its own limited, primarily tactical, role in stimulating ethical thinking, whereas three of the four predecessor ICAS reports on ethics have been literature reviews with a more strategic focus.

Nevertheless, the report concludes that with professional ethics, a profound, enduring, and yet changing challenge is that each individual within each generation needs, at least periodically and perhaps even continuously, to keep 'exploring' issues of ethics, each for themselves. The benefit of all this 'exploring' is not just for its own sake, but must also become apparent in widespread public use across the multiple activities that accountants straddle. Hopefully, too, along the way, practitioners and other interested readers can enjoy, or at least find stimulating, the potential ethical challenges in addressing the questions of *What do you do now?*

1 Introduction

Rationale and context

The principal purpose of the project underlying this report has been to prepare, without compromising the needs of confidentiality, a series of detailed case-studies or scenarios that are closely based on the real-life experiences of Chartered Accountants in facing what they have seen as ethical issues. Additionally, related commentaries have been prepared for each scenario to draw out possible ways whereby these issues might be addressed. Some common and recurring themes, including seeing the combined 'Guardian' and 'Commercial' functions of accountants, have been identified and explained. The significance of ethical courage, coping with the loneliness of decision-making, and the importance of conscience, of self-discipline and of the development of discernment, are each described briefly in the conclusions.

As the fifth in a series of ICAS research reports on ethics, this project has deliberately not sought to replicate the more overtly academic gathering of statistical evidence or the literature-based approaches of its predecessors. Rather, it seeks to build on their foundations and to serve as a complement to their earlier reviews within the diverse arena of what is meant by 'professional ethics' within accountancy. It is intended also to provide a link to practical educational needs, at both student and CPD levels, consistent with the requirements identified by the International Accounting Education Standards Board (IAESB 2007) to fit within a wider framework.[1]

The report's aim fits with long traditions that any exploration and research on ethical themes must quite determinedly seek to culminate in what is useful in practice. Hence, Epicurus, founder of a subsequent major strand of philosophy, some 2,300 years ago, wrote:

> *Empty is that philosopher's argument by which no human suffering is therapeutically treated. For just as there is no use in a medical art that does not cast out sickness of the body, so too there is no use in philosophy, unless it casts out suffering of the soul.*

Moreover, the underlying methodology of using case-studies, or short narratives, to enlighten understanding and encourage more ethical conduct is ancient too, such as outlined by Megone (2002, pp161-173). Evidence of an independent story - or 'parable' - being deployed to challenge an individual in order to make a serious ethical point dates back at least 2,700 years. Then, according to the Hebrew Bible, the fearsome King David was told by the prophet Nathan about a simple but imaginary incident that loosely paralleled one of his own abuses of regal power. Not realising how his own past conduct had mirrored that described, the monarch denounced the story's main character and decreed retributory justice. When the matching was shown, with the dramatic retort '*You are that man!*', he was, in effect, self-condemned and self-compelled to see his actions from a new perspective.[2]

Such narratives have an enduring power to press individuals to confront issues relating their own characters and actions. Notably, the prophet did not prescribe what an appropriate response might be. Crucially, then as now, it is the listeners, readers or 'thinkers' who must determine the issues and examine the possible solutions, each for themselves.

While this report cannot claim anything as profound or spectacular as either of these foundational models, it is based on the assumption that studying ethics should, ultimately, have a practical end. Without the intention, even if remote, of being some form of contribution to engagement with real issues and dilemmas, writings about ethics would be largely sterile exercises, providing limited edification, except for the author alone. Accessibility, to link theory and practice is, therefore, essential. Within accessibility, a sense of authenticity is important. To be meaningful to practitioners, stories about professional ethics in a specific field - in this instance accountancy - need to have a resonance and credibility related to their own experiences.

To achieve this rapport, it has been necessary to undertake original research. But in reporting that research a potential problem arises: it is necessary to respect the natural wish for privacy of those involved, particularly as often the circumstances involve a client of a CA, for whom there is an established ethical responsibility for maintaining confidentiality. Moreover, some of the more challenging dilemmas involve conflicts of interest between several clients. Ensuring anonymity and permitting adaptation become a prerequisite within the reporting process without distorting the validity of the original circumstances.

The scenarios that form the core to this research are, therefore, a mixture of what volunteer practitioners have been willing to disclose, together with an amalgam of wider experience. This has required altering the contexts, industries and personalities to make the specific experience general, while retaining sufficient detail to give the situation piquancy. To this end, a scenario may incorporate material from more than one source. Inevitably, sometimes, the decision as to what to leave out was often as difficult as determining what to include.

As the research progressed, certain style guidelines were adopted to give uniformity and to emphasise the sharpness of the dilemmas faced. Each scenario is focused on 'you' and at the end the requirement is for 'you' now to make a decision and do something - although a valid option may be for 'you' to decide, consciously, to do nothing. The purpose of this, as with the Socratic approach of probing and questioning, is deliberately to push readers to engage. Your opinions matter; the problem has been made yours, not someone else's.

This style may not fit comfortably with the preferred academic stance of acting as a neutral, objective observer. Yet, without some means of conveying the 'pain' of difficult ethical decision-making, the essence of the research would be still further neutered. The reader (or 'thinker') would have still less need to engage with the experience. Even so, there is still a presentational gulf. By their compressed nature and artificial circumstances, the scenarios cannot readily convey the stealthy onset and often-protracted nature of the problems; the nagging worries and the loneliness that participants may face, perhaps particularly those working outside of accountancy practices.

Yet, if this suggests grounds for paranoia, that too would be misleading. With the scenarios all grouped together, and, if they are read immediately one after another, might come the impression that all accountants are somehow doomed to wander in a perpetual ethical maze, facing crisis after crisis. To counter this, it seems important to quote one respondent who could reply, after 30 years in the profession, covering auditing, insolvency and tax and working at different levels in both small and the largest of firms that:

> *It is fair to say that I have never had any serious ethical moments (perhaps ignorance was bliss!) but one or two examples of issues do occur to me…*

Hence, it is necessary for readers to bear in mind that the plural of 'anecdote' is not 'data'. This study was not seeking to reproduce the more structured exercise of *Taking Ethics to Heart* (ICAS, 2004) that, most usefully, undertook a statistically validated survey showing how issues could present themselves at different career stages. Rather this report offers material that should stimulate the reader 'to think'; 'to share' and 'to discuss'. By gaining, in advance, a shared understanding of what may arise, each individual or group achieves an advantage. He, she or they can prepare to respond for themselves to ethical challenges, or to be able to give advice should a colleague encounter circumstances that are similar - although never quite the same because some factors will always be subtly different and bring different implications.

This, perhaps, raises the important question of 'what is specifically an 'ethical' issue?' - as opposed to, say, an 'audit technical', or a 'human sensitivity', issue? No contributor opted to include choosing between complicated technicalities. It may be a limitation of this report that it does not attempt to take an unequivocal stance. Rather, as so much with ethics, the answer will depend upon the approach taken by the reader or 'thinker'.

Moreover, although definitions and terminology should help clarify rational thinking around the problem, what actually matters is not the description 'ethical'. It is that the key parties are identified; critical issues prioritised and an appropriate response delivered to the overall situation, in keeping with the profession's foundational principles of 'integrity', 'objectivity', 'diligence', 'competence', 'confidentiality' and a sense of 'public service'. If these attributes are evident in how an accountant instinctively 'does' - approaches and delivers - all aspects of, say, 'tax' or 'audit', then classifying an issue as 'technical' rather than 'ethical' is of lesser importance.

Legal considerations

Emphasis throughout the report is given to 'principles' and significantly less to citing 'regulations'. This is not to diminish the importance of specific requirements, such as The Terrorism Act 2000, the Proceeds of Crime Act 2002, the Money Laundering Regulations of 2003 and subsequent, or the Serious Organised Crime and Police Act 2005 that might impact on readers working in the UK. Clearly, in considering the relationship of law and ethics a significant feature is the fact that the principle of 'confidentiality' is not always sacrosanct but subject to modification in some statutorily-determined circumstances. Hence the legislation has specific obligations such as the need to send 'suspicious activity reports' to a national criminal intelligence service (currently for the UK the Serious Organised Crime Agency), whilst taking care to avoid 'tipping off'.

Whilst these regulations may have added to tensions in practitioner/client/new client relationships, they may, as intended, have also simplified the decision process for accountants faced with evidence giving rise to suspicion of financial irregularities. There is a stipulated duty to report such, although not speculation. The distinctions may often be subtle so that the need for specialist guidance is essential for proper understanding. However, this report is not a training manual. It does not spell out the precise regulatory requirements for any jurisdiction nor provide any form of legal precedents.

This is not to deny the fact that difficulties for legal compliance will have ethical dimensions. Deciding to adhere to an ethical principle may sometimes bring an unavoidable clash with legal stipulations. Such situations are nothing new. To cite another ancient example, some 2,460 years ago, exploration of such a theme was at the heart of Sophocles' play, Antigone. The stark choice for the heroine was either respecting traditional familial funerary duties or complying with legal civic demands that denied these for those deemed traitors. On pain of punishment she decided to disobey the law. Agonising over such conflicts remains an enduring feature of drama and of narratives that spill over into real life.

One way to try to lessen the drama within professional and business life is to make decisions always based on the best possible levels of information. This will include information about current expectations and legal interpretations. Obtaining specific legal advice is necessary in challenging circumstances. Thereafter, the practitioner will still have to make and implement decisions, taking account of ethical considerations. In rare instances, integrity may require going against the rules or letter of the law. But, in reaching any such decision, the ethical demands of objectivity, competence, diligence and public duty must also have been fully exercised. Clearly, trying to predict precisely how and when to use legal advice, and especially when to override such advice, will vary, making this area beyond the scope of this report. Hence, in the scenarios and their analysis, legal references have deliberately been kept to a minimum.

So, too, in analysing each of the scenarios, core consideration has been given to the five fundamental principles set out in the ICAS Code of Ethics, adopted in November 2006, which follows closely the IFAC Code of Ethics that serves as the model on which national ethical guidance is based. Reference has not been made to the ethical pronouncements of other specific bodies such as, for example, the Ethical Standards for Auditors issued by the UK Auditing Practices Board. By adopting a highest level, principles-only, approach the emphasis is on the global and enduring nature of the issues that arise for individuals' experiences.

The historical vision of ethics for accountants

Yet, as a few of the scenarios illustrate, recent tightened confidential reporting regulations have probably sharpened the acuteness of some decision-making. More broadly, it raises a fundamental question as to when the role of an accountant, as being an entrepreneurial 'Commercial' operator required to service the needs of business and organisations, transfers across to being that of a more orderly 'Guardian'. This is a complex theme that requires more explanation. As well as considering these two functions under each scenario, this mode of viewing the role is picked up separately both in chapter three and in the conclusions.

The requirements of accounting and of ethics pervade, and, therefore, must be integrated into almost every human activity. Hence a breadth of vision is required, as has been recognised since the origins of accountancy as a profession. Notably, the petition for the Incorporation by the Royal Charter by the Society of Accountants of Edinburgh in 1854 stated:

> *Accountants* [in specific capacities] *have duties to perform, not only of the highest responsibility... but which require, in those who*

undertake them, great experience of business, very considerable knowledge of law and other qualifications that can only be obtained by a liberal education.

In short, in both the past and today, respecting an understanding of commercial business, guarding the law and using judgement derived from wider experiences when tackling difficult ethical dilemmas, are integral parts of being a professional accountant.

Endnotes

1. Following IAESB usage, the terms 'ethics' and 'ethical' have been used exclusively throughout the report rather than 'morality' and 'moral' except where there is a deliberate contrast. Some writers and speakers make a distinction between 'ethics' as relating to character or culture (as in ethos) and 'morality' as relating to actions (as in mores), which follows their Greek and Latin derivations.

2. Second Book of Samuel, Chapter 12, verses 1-15. The king had organised for the deliberate death in battle of a husband whose wife he himself had seduced and wished to marry. The prophet told a hypothetical story of a wealthy man taking a poor man's lamb to make a meal for a visiting traveller, prompting the king's outrage and subsequent realisation of his own abuse of power.

2 The Methodologies of Research and Analysis

Introduction

The four earlier ICAS reports on ethics have picked up on the larger, more strategic issues of ethics and of professional accountants in practice within firms and in business. Three of the four were specifically designated, within their titles, as reviews of the relevant literature. The research for this report had a distinctly different purpose. It is to concentrate on the more immediate, tactical or local issues and to explore:

- some specific ethical challenges encountered by practising accountants;
- how individual (and sometimes painfully-acquired) experiences can be shared appropriately with other accountants, at different stages of their careers, to enhance the collective abilities of the profession in tackling ethical challenges; and
- the insights that can be gained through an analysis of the material that might help develop ethical awareness among accountants.

Methods of research

Given the research aims noted above, the three underlying tasks of this project were as follows. Firstly, to listen as accountants described circumstances encountered during their practice when they had to make a decision which, in their opinion, had an ethical dimension.

Secondly, to reproduce these in a form that protected confidentialities whilst conveying something of the issues faced. The third, and perhaps the most difficult part, was to try to analyse and explain in a reasonably accessible and methodical way how a reader might reach a conclusion as to what might be appropriate as current best practice.

The first task was to gather the experiences as raw data. Although recourse might, perhaps, have been made to disciplinary records of ethical infringements, the material likely to emerge from that source would inevitably be that of more egregious breaches, such as had triggered complaints. While interesting, it would not be representative. Less extreme and more general challenges, but challenges nonetheless, would need to be discovered through voluntary access. Hence the methodology adopted needed to persuade individuals to make recollections and to discuss what most would probably have preferred to forget.

Following two pilot interviews, the initial approach to collection was to publicise the project generally, through the CA Magazine and other channels. However, in that this, predictably, produced only one contact, the researcher asked individual acquaintances directly if they would be willing to participate. Most of those approached, but not all, agreed, albeit sometimes with delay and reluctance. The initial promotion had served a useful purpose in being a reference point. It was also a form of confirmation that it would be ethically appropriate to reveal something of otherwise confidential circumstances.

These 'volunteers' were then interviewed in informal settings with the core purpose that they should share their memories of incidents with an ethical dimension that they judged had impacted upon them. Such notes as the researcher took were necessarily informal. Electronic recording in order to prepare transcripts would have seemed at variance with the assurance that the interviewee's 'story' would be altered and anonymised.

These notes were used to prepare a first draft of a scenario which was then sent for comment within two or three working days. Interviewees were asked to make comments and to advise if they felt any reservation over giving an affirmative answer to the question:

> *Based on your own experience as a Chartered Accountant, is the situation described a realistic and credible scenario?*

Given the aims of the research, this question was fundamental. Testing the validity of the research product by this means was of far more importance than trying to adhere to a methodology that required details to be replicated as closely as possible while also being confidential. Sometimes it was the researcher's own experience/imagination that changed the industry. Otherwise, there were opportunities for maintaining anonymity through mixing and matching. Some interviewees had more than one 'story'. Sometimes, a 'story' from one interview fitted closely with a similar scenario outlined by another person. Hence, details from two different sources could sometimes be woven together to form one scenario. These techniques seemed valid in order to maintain the essential confidentiality.

Interviewees were not pressed to give details of how the problems were resolved, particularly as to what had been their own initiatives, or inactions. Some chose to describe the outcome but, unlike a tribunal or disciplinary committee, it was not part of the research process to seek confessions, to criticise, or offer some third party judgement.

To have made criticisms or to imply a verdict during any part of the research process could have discouraged most volunteers from any further frank disclosure. Nevertheless, it was reassuring to the robustness of the process when, in some instances, interviewees did acknowledge that, with hindsight, action or inaction on their part could have achieved a more ethically-justifiable outcome. Occasionally, these comments are featured at the end of the analyses. Overall, the primary concern is not what someone else did, or did not do, but what the readers themselves make of each scenario.

Given the situation described above, inevitably, the resulting 28 scenarios are not the memories of a representative cross-section of the profession as a whole. Rather they constitute the self-selected stories of selected individuals who were willing to tell. Also, some of the selection from their memories will already have been consciously, or unconsciously, filtered. However, care was taken to gain a balanced mix of gender, size of current employers (whether in industry or in practice), commercial or not-for-profit work contexts, size of interviewees' original training firms, and to cover each of the major specialities such as tax, audit, insolvency and consultancy/advisory services. Getting a spread of ages proved more difficult in that interviewees were currently aged between 30 to mid 60's. Nevertheless, students and 'under 30s' were represented, if only indirectly, in that several interviewees recalled experiences from earlier stages of their careers.

The research's limitations and potential, and use of the term 'scenario'

It could be argued that these methods have followed relatively loosely the principles set out by Yin (2003) for case study research but they have been adapted pragmatically to fit the purposes of the research and to present the findings appropriately to the particular circumstances. For this, the role of narrative is important and could be the subject of much further description and debate for, as Llewellyn (1999, p220) noted:

> *Narrating is a mode of thinking and persuading that is as legitimate as calculating, but as a mode of thinking, it has been under-utilized in the social sciences.*

This legitimacy is echoed by Michael Porter (2006, pp1-2), the Harvard professor widely celebrated for the originality and insightfulness of his research on strategy and competition. Speaking of the academic discipline of management, into which research and teaching on professional or business ethics might most naturally fit, he claims:

> *Our field is inherently complex and multidimensional. It is a field where you simply cannot learn all there is to learn about the field by simply developing models. These models take a limited view of the world, or just doing statistical work, which is constrained by the data that you have available or can easily assemble.*

Such complexity seems true also for ethics. Porter goes on to opine:

> *... we have to find ways of capturing the complexity of management. And the only way we can do that is with in-depth, longitudinal, carefully crafted, rigorously developed case studies.*

With the exploration of any issue, the longitudinal requirement will be necessary if, retrospectively, the longer term consequences have to be known in order to inform the analysis. In this way the positives and negatives can be calculated, compared and the benefits of hindsight gleaned by future managers. But by the nature of ethical issues, the specifics of an outcome for a singular set of circumstances may point only very rarely to what should become an unalterable precedent for the future. Therefore, developing the personal processes to discern the most appropriate decision, within the limited knowledge available, is the more important lesson, as too is understanding the difficulty and pain of having to make and implement some decisions.

Hence, while recognising the necessity of following the techniques for business case-study preparation, these ethical 'case-studies' are presented differently, acknowledging that for the most part they lack the longitudinal element. That is not to say that the problems presented may not have been long in development but the need has become for a prompt and early decision. What might have happened next is not revealed because it is the reader's own response that now matters most. To indicate this difference from more conventional business case-studies, the term 'scenario' has been adopted by the author for use throughout this report.

What may seem surprising is the relative absence of specific accountancy-related ethical issues (as opposed to ethical issues for accountants) that emerged from the interviews. This may be because the contributors, instinctively, saw these more as technical features of their work, or else as deeper, profession-wide concerns requiring more societal, theoretical, or textbook exploration than linked to individual incidents. This is not to suggest that the disciplines of accountancy do not generate ethical dilemmas. Fortunately, for this research project, some compensation for any such omissions can be found in the four ICAS reports earlier in the series. Deliberately, there has been minimal duplication of their content or in citing references already covered within these.

In short, the intended application for these scenarios is that they should be used for personalised reflections and also be available for collective discussion as part of accountancy education. This applies also to the accompanying analyses. Like the scenarios, these are much more to prompt reactions from you, the reader, than to present what someone unknown has, or has not, decided, or what some remote committee might prescribe. Rather, the emphasis is on prompting learning from personal engagement with the research. Nevertheless, it is hoped that the author's insights, drawn from a familiarity gathered over many months, may serve as a useful starting point for each reader's own further potential probing of the problems presented. Ultimately, all of the material is to serve as a resource for readers to use as seems most appropriate and helpful for themselves.

Methods of analysis

The process method of the analysis of the scenarios could have drawn from many possible inspirations. This is perhaps best illustrated by summarising different sources representing a spectrum between academic and informal practice.

- From an academic perspective, Maclagan (2003), drawing on many years of teaching business ethics, set out a seven step framework of exploring, mostly retrospectively, case-studies of varying sizes. These emphasised the importance of: identifying the ethical agents; whether there was an actual dilemma (involving a conflict of ethical values rather than just 'ethical issues' or 'conflicts of interests' in a 'quasi dilemma'); the variety of possible ethical theories; and ethical imagination.
- *Taking Ethics to Heart* (2004, p60) suggested a systemic model for practical decision-making involving the drawing together of five sets of criteria, based on social norms, attitudes and volition controls, within an overall framework
- The *ICAEW Additional Guidance on Ethical Matters for Members in Business* (2004) also suggested a seven step process linked to testing against the foundational ethical principles of accountancy the identification of facts, affected parties and participants and various courses of action. This guidance illustrates these with 10 short case studies and outlines for each of a 'possible course of action'.
- At a late stage in the preparation of this report, *Integrity at Work in Financial Services* was published by the Securities and Investment Institute (2007). It is a practical guide to trust and integrity dilemmas, providing what is termed a 'Quick read summary' of 14 case-studies drawn from the financial services sector. This asks the reader to identify, 'What is/would be ethical'; 'Key points'; 'Adverse consequences'; 'Optimum approach'; and 'SII Code of Conduct impact' for cross referral to its seven principles.

- *The Integrity Compass* (2005), which is a 'game' developed by Deloitte, loosely based on 'Trivial Pursuits' but a very imaginative means of integrating ethical awareness into training processes. It proposes five questions, namely: 'What is the ethical problem?', 'Which information do I need to make a decision?', 'Which arguments are relevant?', 'How do the ethical principles and shared values impact on my decision?' and 'What is my decision or action?' KPMG too has a game, 'Cards on the Table', to open up discussions on ethical dilemmas in work settings.

What is readily apparent is that there is a high level of commonality between these sources but with different ways and sequences for posing similar questions. In this project, the way the scenarios have been presented is to pose the question 'what do you do now?' This question, presented at the end of quite long narratives, has sought to minimise the need for more information or more extensive identification of the ethical agents (as required by Maclagan).

Revisions to the ethical guidelines in 2006 that increased recognition of the importance of professional behaviour, as being for the 'public interest' within the statement of fundamental principles, have heightened that aspect of expected obligations. For the analysis, the need was to find a combination of questions that could be applied methodically; would be suitably rigorous and searching and yet be readily accessible without too much academic or philosophical jargon. It also needed to be tailored to the specific features of the accountancy professions and its particularly selected principles. Hence, the framework for analysis adopted by the author during the course of the research has drawn from each of these sources to ask questions, as follows:

(1) What are the readily-identifiable ethical issues for your decision?

(2) Who are the key parties (including 'you') who can influence, or will be affected by, your decision?

(3) What fundamental ethical principles for accountants are most applicable and is there an apparent conflict between them?

(4) Is there any further information (including legal obligations) or discussion that might be relevant?

(5) Is there a conflict between the 'Guardian' and 'Commercial' strands of an accountant's responsibilities?

(6) Based on the information available, is there scope for an imaginative solution?

(7) Are there any other comments?

Within question one, there is a differentiation between 'for you personally' and 'for the CA firm' where the scenario is set in professional practice. In some ways this sustains the approaches in the earlier reports of Ken McPhail (2006) and Aileen Pierce (2007) and reflects the hope that distinguishing between 'personal' and 'the firm' perspectives may be helpful for the analysis. However, the over-riding intention remains to emphasise that, ultimately, the ethical decisions are personal and individual. Whatever the apparent vice-like grip of organisational expectations and constraints, a core freedom of humans remains to choose one's own attitude in any given set of circumstances. Fundamental to the framework of this research report is that it should encourage each potential reader to be able to think, to decide and, if necessary, to act independently as a professional.

The tentative nature of the analysis

The project has not extended the stages further to imply any form of 'model answer'. Initially, that may appear to be akin to ethical cowardice on the part of the researcher! However, to do so would seem both to claim an unwarranted authority and be self-defeating to the aims of the research. Firstly, the formal Guidance prepared in collaboration with other member bodies of the Consultative Committee of Accountancy Bodies offers only 'possible courses of action' for its cases. Secondly, suggesting that an apparently definitive answer actually exists could kill off discussion. Rather, the purpose of collecting and publishing the cases is to promote critical thinking and wider debate so that individuals and groups tease out for themselves what they might do in such circumstances. Thirdly, and more realistically, ambiguity rather than perfection can be expected. It is entirely consistent with an approach to accountancy that emphasises pursuing principles rather than adhering to rules, that understanding the application of professional ethics should be more by way of exploration than looking for prescriptive and exclusively 'right' answers.

The goal of the exploration can best be illustrated by referral to the aspiration in the Four Quartets of T.S. Eliot (1944, p48):

We shall not cease from exploration
And the end of all our exploring
Will be to arrive where we started
And know the place for the first time.

Little Gidding, 239-42

3 The 'Guardian' and 'Commercial' Ethical Syndromes

Introducing the concept

In the predecessors of this series, Alan Lovell (2005) looked at literature relating to business ethics, in contrast to the subsequent focus on accountants' professional ethics for individuals by McPhail (2006) and for firms by Pierce (2007). This split reflected the broader context of a burgeoning interest in ethics amongst those working in commercial enterprises. Moreover, other professions are seeking to codify an approach to conduct and values by their members. For example, under UN auspices, in 2003 the 'Bangalore Principles' of Judicial Conduct were initiated as a common set of concepts for assimilation by judges and for the delivery of justice internationally. 'Judicial Independence', 'Impartiality of process and decision', 'Integrity', 'Competence' and 'Diligence' mirror remarkably closely the principles supported by the International Federation of Accountants (IFAC). However, there are a few subtle differences of emphasis, notably for personal relationships and avoidance of any perceived bias, hence stipulations such as 'the Equality of treatment for all before the Court' and 'Propriety and the appearance of Propriety in activities outside of the Court'.

Such circumstances raise the question as to why there could not yet be a single, universally-accepted code of ethical expectations for all professionals, regardless as to specialisation, across a spectrum that might include, say, judges, police, the military, the clergy, teachers, politicians, actuaries, insurance sellers, engineers, consultants, purchasing managers, journalists, estate agents, taxi-drivers and traders (be it of foreign exchange or used cars). It might be objected that some of these groups are not professionals. Yet, all the practitioners have the commonalities of being human and, through technical knowledge and competence, they provide necessary contributions to the workings of society.[1]

The fact that this single, trans-professional and intra-business code does not yet exist, invites the prospect that through understanding what might be prioritised, included or excluded by one group of specialists as to its professional ethical aspirations, might come insights for those operating elsewhere. Such insights, particularly of the interpretation into practice, would seem useful for those whose functions combine elements of several tasks. This includes many accountants who, when acting as auditors, have duties and formal roles that are like those of judges and are based on law. They issue opinions in a quasi-judicial manner yet receive their remuneration at times through processes of negotiation and haggling more akin to commodity trading. The low-balling of audit fees might be deemed professionally unethical and dangerous but, elsewhere, discounting the cost of providing goods or services has no such stigma. Moreover, many accountants both train and work outwith an audit context.

Competition and the stimulus of more efficient practices may sometimes be seen as ethical and beneficial, yet sometimes not. Trying to understand 'why' and 'when' has been a particular feature of the analysis of the scenarios. Probing such questions may enhance understanding of the underlying ambiguities of a profession that calls simultaneously for the exercise of impartial judgement and caution but also encourages its members to complement the commercial awareness, acumen, accessibility to ideas and creativity of their commercial clients. For many, such attributes are expected too by their employers. Sitting at the cusp between regulation and enterprise creates a dynamic but ethically-paradoxical milieu. To be able to place themselves within this, accountants need to explore the foundations of the societal systems in which they operate.

Different roles and different interpretations of ethical values

Some of the features for different combinations of values for practitioners of varied functions in society were identified by the social anthropologist, Jane Jacobs (1992). She did so through the traditional philosopher's medium of a devised dialogue amongst a fictional group. This presents the arguments in an engaging way and more readily reflects the inevitable variances and exceptions. Whilst it can make for a loss of clarity or an absence of readily citable quotations, the broad tenets of Jacobs' proposition are not hard to follow - that there are twin foundations for ethical values, those of 'Guardians' and those of 'Commerce'.

Because traders, who follow 'Commerce', invariably deal with those who can go elsewhere (either immediately or by choosing not to return with repeat business), they will be more willing to value the ability to come to voluntary agreements. It is sensible to compromise with counter-parties, be they customers or suppliers. By contrast, judges, the ultimate arbiters as to the 'Guardian' role of law, have no need to negotiate or mediate. They deliver judgements of innocence or guilt and pronounce terms of punishment on counter-parties who come before them, sometimes being brought forcibly and only very rarely through choice or for pleasure. The circumstances are fundamentally different. Judges should not be looking for future relationships. For guidance as to their decisions, judges will be more cautiously concerned with the precedents of elite groups of other judges who have historically received the respect of their peers. By further contrast, for traders, the extension of contracts, the innovations of strangers, inventiveness, thrifty investment and efficiencies are likely to be more attractive. Most fundamentally, pay arrangements for judges should be overtly different from those of the open markets.

Jacobs (1992) points to a still wider range of possible differences. 'Guardians' - with often militaristic or regulatory duties - will be more exclusive and less open to fraternising outside of their own circle. For the benefits of security and personal safety they are likely to place high value on obedience to orders, loyalty and honour. Hierarchy is therefore more important, along with attributes such as ostentatious displays of power; willingness to enforce and accept discipline; to refuse to compromise and to seek vengeance; to strike pre-emptively or to deceive and ambush for the sake of the task. 'Guardian' attitudes to what can, or cannot, be approved may be stark. Unbridled mercenary motives are likely to be especially despised, but 'Guardians' will tend to shun the demands of 'Commercial' operators who would more naturally prefer widespread collaboration with aliens; independent exploration of ideas and possibilities; the promotion of comfort and convenience and respect for contracts based on mutual trading benefits.

Implications of distinguishing the functions

This short account may seem merely to offer simplistic stereotypes. Resurrecting reference to the antipathy to trading by past aristocracies that concentrated solely on state governance, the military and the security of farming to produce food (but not for themselves to sell) may seem primitive. Moreover, the existence of pure 'Guardian' and 'Commerce' is blurred by the symbiotic nature of their relationships. Nevertheless, the outline of the functions is apparent. 'Guardians' need to provide and secure the environment and social infrastructure wherein 'Commerce' can flourish. Prosperity in turn benefits the 'Guardians' in a positive spiral. Mutual respect and co-operation combined in a creative tension is a shared interest, although those in 'Commerce' may need to tolerate the 'Guardian's' pre-dispositions to exalt their own status and to polarise their own activities as more important.

Within sophisticated societies the transfer of understanding of the different attributes and mindsets will happen frequently. But dangers may still emerge where those from 'Guardian' traditions seek to run business activities using their own perceptions as to priorities (e.g. government representatives running a theme park). Conversely, tensions arise when those whose past experience is mostly of enterprising 'Commerce' are given powers and resources to run on 'businesslike lines' what are widely (and often emotively) perceived as predominantly 'Guardian' functions (e.g. some public services in security, health or education). To avoid the misunderstanding of core considerations, as with even the simplest of accounting systems, some respect for the division of duties is essential, with a 'doer' and a 'checker' necessary for internal controls, although each must have some appreciation of the other's role.

Clearly, there will always be risks for strategic activities in society if, due to confusion, the 'Guardian' and 'Commercial' foundations of ethical priorities come to support inappropriate functions. Some prohibitions may be inevitable. At its most basic, judges should not be settling a commercial judgement by reference to a tariff of bids (or bribes) from the disputant parties. But too many absolute bans on transfer and experimentation would risk stifling a vibrant society. The creative nature of the risks may benefit the workings of a hybrid activity - such as the provision of a professional audit service through independent accountants and their firms. But to help with the preservation of a balance of risks and to recognise the importance of sustaining the nexus of trust within society, the auditor needs to be conscious of how the 'Guardian' and 'Commercial' roles both compete for his or her ethical attention.

Like judges, auditors must exercise skill and judgement. But unlike judges, auditors have a further, major professional requirement, first to establish and then to sustain a good working relationship with those affected by their verdicts. As noted above, beyond common courtesy, judges have no cause to show any such companionability.

Indeed, to develop friendly familiarity with parties to a dispute, with witnesses or with those accused, would cause alarm among advocates and fellow judges. By contrast, auditors, needing to please, become far more vulnerable, should those subject to their judgements choose to go 'opinion-shopping'. Technically, it may be the shareholders at an AGM who appoint the auditors but, in reality, the directors and management of a company make a single recommendation, and hence the decision. Thus, it is not difficult to foresee the pressures on impartiality for an auditor that may arise if, say, the size of the directors' remuneration (whether in terms of bonuses or the value of share options) is highly dependent on some subjective decisions in relation to the reporting of profits.

Despite what might seem a compelling case for separation there are sound arguments for such arrangements. Unlike with 'one-off' court cases, a mass of financial statements require an annual opinion. Timely-reporting and efficiency are essentials for reporting and for finance, so that auditors justifiably face similar commercial pressures as their clients, in being forced to operate in lean and risk-based ways that enhance the usefulness of their role. Moreover, to attract and sustain clients there is a compulsion to be relevant and knowledgeable about those clients' specific industrial sectors.

But the strengths of giving accountants incentives to become familiar with, and trusted by, clients may turn into risks if this brings over-closeness and undue dependency. Hence, through the fusing together of 'Guardian' and 'Commercial' functions, the office of auditor requires that accountants often practise with an unusually high level of ethical risk, hence also a very conscious self-control (Molyneaux, 2003).

To fortify such self-control for those in such a cross-over role, society traditionally imposed a legal structure for auditors that would leave them jointly and severally open to the severe threat of unlimited liability through litigation. This represents a 'Commercial' sanction with

'Commercial' scale penalties. By contrast, some statutory immunity from such pursuit has been available for 'Guardians' (such as judges or - in the past - advocates). Irrespective of whether in either Government or 'Commercial' posts, very few employees (as opposed to self-employed partners) have lived with any risk of direct punitive action against their personal assets for failures by themselves or colleagues. If erring, their punishment may have been through loss of office, of earnings and of reputation - but not also the risk of potential personal bankruptcy, even if relatively rare in practice.

It is beyond the scope of this report to enter the long-standing and multi-faceted debate as to the fairness or otherwise of unlimited liability as a device for enforcing a discipline on auditors. Moreover, the exact extent of its impact on an individual auditor's ethical scruples is probably unknowable, perhaps even (or maybe especially) to those for whom it has been a formative part of their experience. Suffice it to note the intention. For those spanning both of the 'Guardian' and 'Commercial' syndromes, temptations to exploit the ethically-sensitive status of the role of auditor must be robustly deterred. They should have a powerful inducement to encourage each other to develop diligence, caution and self-restraint.

Significance of the risks and opportunities of accountancy ethics

Systemic ethical risk and the obligation of accountants to respect the public interest extends beyond auditors. It has implications also for those working in industry, business or consulting, in insolvency, in taxation, in advisory practice or in public, or 'not-for-profit', administration. The significance of this spreads even more widely than for most professionals in that accounting in monetary terms, like ethics, is an essential for every organisation, where accountancy requirements are found ubiquitously, rather than in silos.

If 'death' and 'taxes' are the two certainties of an individual's life, arguably, the two necessities for any organisation seeking to exist in perpetuity are 'ethos' and 'accounting'. Potentially, this pervasiveness can be positive. Some accountants may work with social workers and some accountants with merchant bankers, even if the other two types of professional would rarely mix, except by chance. The ethics of accountants will, therefore, tend to straddle and be compared with those of other disciplines in a manner that creates particular responsibilities and opportunities for accountants. The bankers and the social workers may have sharply different views on an identical scenario about the ethical requirements of, say, extending credit to young people. Accountants, as a profession with a long history of 'seeking truth' and 'finding balance', may have a role in moderating or explaining risks. Interpreting for others ethical demands and expectations may be as useful as interpreting for them financial and operational data, although the potential threats of litigation may act as a deterrent for accountants from venturing into some innovative, but less-well defined, areas.

In analysing each of the scenarios, there is the specific question: is there a conflict between the 'Guardian' and 'Commercial' strands of an accountant's responsibilities? It is there not because it alters the underlying principles of integrity, objectivity, competence, diligence and confidentiality. Nor does it provide any simple means for discerning a solution to fit public service. Rather it is a prism for seeing the interpretations and expectations that come from each activity. Inevitably, the question brings into sharp focus that views on what constitutes 'professional behaviour' will often differ.

This could be dismissed as a dangerous relativism. Nevertheless, posing this question seems a useful feature for pragmatic understanding of the nature of the ethical problem. It places an onus on professionals to explore alternative views. The corollary of 'I know what my ethics tell me is right', may be 'I can see too that your different suggestion may be right also'. This is not to condone what should widely be condemned as ignored conflicts of interest or flouted conventions. Rather, it holds open that through discussion over difficult dilemmas, there may be clearer thinking and challenge amongst groups who, by their examples, actually set standards.

There is a further factor. Appreciating the duality within the accounting role could help to address lowered respect within society for accountants through scepticism, an attitude that may of itself lower accountants' ethical aspirations. The depictions have been, and remain, discouraging.

Past generations may have been influenced indirectly by Plato's acerbic censure of Homer, for showing Achilles, otherwise the classic archetype of the noblest hero, demeaning himself as a trader, in that he received gifts in exchange for agreeing to hand over a corpse. In this view, whoever receives payments for their decisions and actions can be bought off and so forfeits a claim to glory. Freedom and independence are at risk. Rather than being heroic, the willingness to engage in barter, to calculate and to take a reward is to suffer from 'the disease of mean-spirited avarice'.[2]

Future generations may continue to harbour a residual sense of such negativity, as can be readily shown by the words of J.K. Rowling (1997, pp 74-75). Large numbers of contemporary children - as well as adults - worldwide may have an impression of accountants influenced by the following exchange between Harry Potter in his first ever conversation with his friend, Ron:

Are all your family wizards?' asked Harry, who found Ron just as interesting as Ron found him.

Er – yes, I think so' said Ron. 'I think Mum's got a second cousin who's an accountant, but we never talk about him.

Whatever the impact of this ignominious image, succinctly and graphically it illustrates a real problem.[3] The nature and contexts of the ethical challenges for accountants - a standing up for principles - that might require serious 'heroism', if not wizardry - need both to be better understood and better explained. First, these must be identified and publicised. Narrative - story-telling - seems a way to begin.

Endnotes

1. For the possible importance of 'competence' as an arbiter of what will constitute 'professionalism' in the 21st Century, see Cheetham & Chivers (2005).

2. Plato, in The Republic, 391, refers to the depiction of Achilles in Homer's The Iliad that predates the age of written narrative.

3. Other professions may fare little better, as in the exchange in Rowling (2007, p105) between the bright heroine and an uninspirational character:

   Are you planning to follow a career in Magical Law, Miss Granger? asked Scrimgeour [the Minister for Magic]

   'No, I am not,' retorted Hermione, *'I'm hoping to do some good in the world'.*

4 The Case Study Scenarios

Using the scenarios

The sequence, in which the scenarios are presented, as set out below, has no major significance. For convenience, an attempt has been made to group the case-studies by their settings (e.g. professional firm, commercial industry, non-profit) and the accountancy discipline (e.g. Audit, Tax, Insolvency) in which the ethical issues arose. However, some involve elements of cross-disciplinary awareness and many of the situations could be encountered in subtly different ways in diverse contexts, irrespective of accountancy, or even any professional specialisation (e.g. scenarios 2, 4, 24 and 25 have almost universal relevance).

The report has been designed so that each scenario and analysis can be read in isolation - save to note that scenario 15 shares the same initial client circumstances as scenario 14, albeit then operating in a different geographical continent. This 'stand-alone' approach should be not only more useful for educational purposes but also, as noted on page 4, anyone reading all 28 without pause for reflection, might get a distorted impression of the challenges that a typical, single accountant might face in a lifetime.

As a further aide to usage, the following index gives some indication of the level at which 'you' are operating within the organisation where the problems have been encountered. However, in that the situations often require consideration of different relationships, this does not mean that the interest need be confined to individuals only at particular stages within a set hierarchy. For example, a relatively junior CA student could well encounter aspects of the circumstances described in scenarios 1, 2, 3, 4, 7, 12, 13, 14, 15, 21, 24, 25, 26 or 28. Moreover, an enquiring or ambitious student may be even more interested at trying to determine the type of demands that could be faced by senior CAs, such as found in scenarios 9, 10, 11, 16, 17, 19, 22 and 23.

The listing of 'Principal ethical issues' tries to summate in a few words what are the dominant themes for each scenario. This may be helpful to determine which might particularly catch a reader's interest. However, readers coming with personal perspectives are likely to concentrate on different features.

Lengths vary, as do the potential consequences and seriousness of the embedded challenges. Each has some element of ambiguity and often one or more complicating twists in the plot that could test a CA's sense of objectivity. This reflects that rarely do ethical challenges come in simple form, and even less often with a convenient label attached stating 'Ethical Dilemma'.

Brief summaries of each scenario's context, level and principal ethical issues

No.	Context and title	Level	Principal ethical issues	Pg.
Professional firm/general practice				
1	Billing for Ernest's cover-up	Partner/manager	Conflicts of interest/ differential recovery rates for billing and client relationships	34
2	The weekend expenses claim	Anyone	'False accounting'/personal integrity	43
3	A student's insights	HR partner/ practice partner/ any CA	'Whistleblowing'/ objectivity and conflicts of interest.	49
4	Temptation at the tender	Partner/any CA	Maintaining personal and collective integrity and objectivity	55
5	Partnership problems	Junior partner	Confidentiality in relation to fellow CAs	63
6	The disaster waiting to happen!	Ethics partner and engagement partner	Confidentiality/possible intervention on behalf of client and conflicts of interest	69
Family business				
7	When cash is king	New financial controller/ company secretary	Contrasting acceptability (or otherwise) of cash transactions, including personal use/'false accounting' and conflicts of interest. Set in the retail industry.	77
8	The directors' unofficial loan account	New financial director in isolated circumstances	'False accounting' and personal conflicts of interest. Set in the hotel industry.	85
9	Unhealthy foods	Audit partner	Confidentiality set in the health food sector	91

No.	Context and title	Level	Principal ethical issues	Pg.
Audit				
10	Foreign corrupt practices	Junior 'salaried' partner	Confidentiality/conflicts of interest in a non-UK context	97
11	Interim results	Established audit partner	Confidentiality and relationships in FTSE 100 context	103
Audit with tax complications				
12	Poor charity!	Partner - any level	Conflicts of interest/ interpretation of tax rules	108
13	Obligations to disclose	Partner/manager	Confidentiality/conflicts of interest	112
Tax practice				
14	Can the 'withholding tax' be recovered?	Partner - international firm. Finance director - private company	'False accounting'/ conflicts of interest and confidentiality	118
15	Should the social security be paid?	Partner - international firm. Finance director - private company	Conflicts of interest and disclosure compliance	123
16	The unwelcome phone call	Partner - sole practice	Confidentiality/conflicts of interest, including public interest	129
Consultancy services				
17	How much do you tell the finance director?	Senior level	Confidentiality/conflicts of interest	133

No.	Context and title	Level	Principal ethical issues	Pg.
Insolvency				
18	Auditor or administrator?	Experienced partner	Regulations, commercial practice and respect for formal records	139
19	Creating 'reservation of title'	Appointed receiver	Conflicts of interest	144
20	Gazumping	Experienced partner/manager	Conflicts of interest, including public interest	149
Public interest				
21	'Dark 'n' stormy'	Experienced CA	Public interest obligations	153
Non profit and recruitment				
22	Quango interview panel	Experienced CA	Confidentiality/public interest obligations	160
23	Recruitment and being a trustee	Experienced CA	Confidentiality/public interest obligations	164
Professional relationships				
24	An alleged intimate relationship	HR partner/any CA	Confidentiality/conflicts of interest/collective integrity	169
25	A fellow partner's alcohol problem	Experienced CA	Personal integrity/conflicts of interest/conduct style with junior/client staff	175
26	Reasonable encouragement or devious deception?	Experienced CA	Personal integrity/conflicts of interest	180
27	A personal reference	Experienced CA	Personal integrity/conflicts of interest	185
28	How much should money matter?	Any CA	Personal integrity/conflicts of interest	189

Scenario 1: Billing for Ernest's cover-up

You are an audit senior manager for a manufacturing client in the FTSE 350 where your firm's working relationships with the Group's long-standing Finance Director, Ernest, are notoriously 'difficult'. Too often, he seems to equate 'compromise' with 'weakness' so that he makes few concessions to his position without protracted negotiations, whether on timetables, interpretation of standards or fees. This can become disconcerting, not just because they seem unnecessarily time-consuming but the outcomes can seem unreasonable too. For example, when, at the last audit, your firm had resolutely insisted on a more conservative valuation of long-term contracts, Ernest had dropped several unsubtle hints that the engagement should be put out early to tender. Frustratingly, to the client's Audit Committee, Ernest's approach seems characterised not as 'difficult' but as, 'principled'.

Some weeks ago, Neil, the engagement partner, asked you to 'sort out' the accountancy and financial statements of a small private company that had been set up a few years ago to make 'artistic' films. This company had been persistently loss making and its one film, which had taken significantly longer to release than expected, had flopped at the box-office. This was despite being more 'adult' than 'artistic'! During the leisurely production process, significant sums seemed to have been spent on hotels and restaurants.

The shareholders and directors of the company are a young film director and the nubile actress who starred in the film. They are 'resting' and have told you that the company too is now dormant and will be wound up. There are just enough funds to cover the costs of this and of residual bills. Apart from a few small grants, the majority of the finance had been by way of loans that will not now be repaid.

You were very surprised to discover that the source of all these loans had been Ernest. He had also given personal guarantees that all trade creditors will be paid.

As requested by Neil, you have worked closely with a colleague in your firm's tax department to progress the efficient submission to H.M. Revenue and Customs (HMRC) of tax computations for the film company. Alongside this, some advice was given personally to Ernest on the idiosyncrasies of tax and film finance. Apparently, he had previously always dealt with his own tax affairs.

At the start of the assignment two separate charge codes, accountancy and tax, were set up for the film company. Time costs for the work, at your firm's normal rates, have amounted to £20,000 for dealing with the accountancy and £4,000 for the tax. Neil has now sent you instructions relating to monthly billings. These include:

- A fee note of £2,000 to be issued to the film company with £2,000 of accountancy time costs written off against it. The accountancy code is then to be closed.
- The residual £18,000 is to be transferred to a 'Special Work' client account of the Group. This already has in it the time costs of £12,000 for an investigation into a stock discrepancy carried out earlier in the year. The partner tells you that the £4,000 of tax time will also be transferred across.
- Two further fee notes to be raised, one for £27,500 addressed to the Group and one for £500 to be sent to Ernest personally at his home address. In all cases the fee notes' descriptions are to be limited to 'agreed professional fees'.

You have asked Neil in person to confirm these arrangements. Clearly very amused, Neil explained that Ernest had funded the film company over the years on the persuasion of the young actress. Ernest now accepts his investment was seriously flawed and that the loans will never be re-paid. He is keen, to the extent legally possible, to minimise further his personal expenditure while gaining any tax advantages available. Moreover, the situation is, for himself, one of considerable potential embarrassment. He wants the maximum discretion. He is now very grateful to the firm for the work done and, after some remarkably swift negotiation, has approved the three billings represented by Neil's instructions. Ernest accepts one further note of fee will be necessary for completing the tax work. This will go to the film company and, as with all the other residual creditors, Ernest will ensure personally that it is paid.

Neil commented that the total billing of £30,000 against incurred costs of £36,000, at 83%, was not as good a recovery as he would have hoped, or might even have negotiated. Yet, this has been his favourite assignment of the summer. He added:

> *I could probably have gone for much higher margins. But I think that it will prove better in the long-term not to have been greedy. Of course, I know Ernest's gratitude won't linger forever. Even so, I think he may be just that bit more co-operative and less aggressive in future. When he reflects that we haven't taken advantage of him and thinks carefully about what we now know, I sense that we will be able to count on his loyalty right through to his retirement! And given how much the old fool has lost on that actress, he'll need to go on working for a good few years yet!*

When you now ask Neil about the ethics of transferring the time costs between clients that have no formal relationship and the apparent subsidy to Ernest personally, he replies:

> *OK, I know that I appear to be charging £27,500 to the Group for an assignment that incurred costs of only £12,000. But the Audit Committee delegated to Ernest the authority to agree fee notes of up to £30,000 for that stock investigation. This time it came in at less. Because of Ernest's attitudes in the past we have*

not been able to recover as much as we should for good work. It's swings and roundabouts.

As for the film company job, I had no real clue from Ernest when we went into it just how heavily he was involved. He said it was primarily a referral to help friends where he has no official, company status. It seemed like useful one-off work when staff members were not busy. Maybe, with hindsight, we wouldn't have taken it. Still, we've tidied up a mess and what the Audit Committee members don't know won't grieve them. Ernest is hardly likely to start revealing all - even if he did with the actress!

Overall, I haven't even pressed for full recovery. No one can tell me the recovery that I have to make on any individual fee note. If I choose, say, zero fee for one piece of work, only 10% for another but 230% for a third, that is my commercial decision.

If this gives you a real problem, just don't transfer time costs between client codes and then don't make any explicit connections. But it will simply be less effort to report one recovery of 100% and one of 82% for our billing department, rather than explaining the detail of 10% here and 200% plus there. The fee income is a done deal; the end result is the same; stand by for a new, more co-operative Ernest!

What do you do now?

Scenario 1: Analysis

What are the readily-identifiable ethical issues for your decision?

For you personally

Do you consider yourself compromised ethically by the initial instructions over billing, such that you need to take alternative action? If so, what action?

For the CA firm

Has an unacceptable conflict of interest arisen from doing, essentially, personal work for a client's FD, even though formally he is neither a shareholder nor officer of the film company?

How do you deal effectively with the sensitivities of billing for professional work and the difficulties of valuing and gaining a perceived 'fair' recovery from a client where there is a determination by the client to haggle over everything?

Can the outcome - while imperfect - be justified on the grounds that the audit firm will be more secure and be able to take a 'tougher' line as auditors in future? Or, is the solution, (of apparent exploitation of a lack of transparency in the billing process) symptomatic of an overall lack of professional integrity in the relationships?

Note: at the time when this occurred there were no formal constraints on providing a personal tax service to, and billing personally, an officer of a corporate client. However, this regulatory detail does not alter the underlying issues. For example, in the scenario described, the token £500 bill for tax and film finance destined for Ernest personally could have been ignored without material financial implications. This charge (or for some other amount) could have been incorporated into the bill sent to the film company for Ernest to settle in full along with residual creditors.

Who are the key parties who can influence, or will be affected by, your decision?

'You', as a senior manager (aspiring partner); Neil as engagement partner; Ernest as commissioner of professional work, negotiator over fees and officer of the company; the Audit Committee as overseer of the process; the Group's stakeholders (including HMRC); the film company's creditors (excluding Ernest).

Which fundamental ethical principles for accountants are most applicable and is there an apparent conflict between them?

Integrity	*Do billing arrangements agreed between Neil and Ernest represent honesty, full truthfulness and fairness?*
Objectivity	*Has the tense relationship with Ernest over fees been replaced with another, if covert, set of dynamics for achieving pragmatic completion of mutual tasks in relation to the company?*
Professional competence and due care	*Assumed*
Confidentiality	*Could the Audit Committee justifiably consider that it should have been informed of the 'new' assignment, once the details of Ernest's involvement were known? By contrast could Ernest justifiably consider that any initiative now by the audit firm to refer to his (indirect) relationship with the film company would be a breach of other expectations of confidentiality?*
Professional behaviour	*Longer term, there could be a loss of respect in an environment where the exchange of 'favours' between auditors and officers, at the apparent expense of others, seems the norm.* *However, in the short and medium term, is Neil's approach towards Ernest and to the billing an instance of where the 'end' of strengthening the auditor's position in relation to an 'awkward character' justifies an opportunistic and dubious 'means'?*

Is there any further information (including legal obligations) or discussion that might be relevant?

Knowing precisely when Neil realised the extent of Ernest's involvement with the film company, hence the possible desirability of the transfer of work to another firm - albeit inefficiently for its winding up and likely to lead to added costs/irritation for Ernest.

More about the working relationship between the Audit Committee and Ernest but in practice you may only ever be able to surmise, rather than know with any certainty, the details.

The skills and integrity of the members of the Audit Committee (or maybe this should make no difference?).

The full extent of the billing and recovery arrangements between the firm and the client, although it can be assumed that £30,000 is significant but not substantial.

Is there a conflict between the 'Guardian' and 'Commercial' strands of an accountant's responsibilities?

Yes. This appears to be a classic instance of a conflict between an accountant's 'Commercial' and 'Guardian' responsibilities.

From a 'Commercial' perspective, you can accept that a compromise is a necessity, if messy. Clearly, some self-interest and fees are needed to keep a firm continuing as auditor. As noted in the opening paragraph, relationships have been strained with Ernest's uncompromising attitudes to negotiation on technical views and on fees. The pragmatic outcome here seems to have provided some benefits to most parties - extra billing/summer work for staff (Neil); a personal problem sorted at lower cost (Ernest); a failed company sorted out with creditor recovery (creditors/public); an increased informal leverage for the auditors over the Finance Director (the firm).

However, the outcome for a 'Guardian' role seems less satisfactory in that the Audit Committee, and through them other stakeholders, appear in this instance to have been hoodwinked through collusion. The Group is paying £27,500 where the auditor's recorded costs are £12,000 (although they were prepared to pay up to £30,000 relying on Ernest to check more precisely). Although the Audit Committee have delegated to the FD responsibility for agreeing fees; the materiality level is more suited for the Group than individuals.

The auditor's future informal leverage over the Finance Director could be open to abuse.

Based on the information available, is there scope for an imaginative solution?

Probably not. Clearly you could 'whistleblow' by retrospectively disclosing the situation directly to the Audit Committee but otherwise 'you' appear to have few options, especially if you act as an individual. Even if your firm contacts the Group's Audit Committee to tell it retrospectively about the film company assignment and the substance (if not the form) of the conflict of interest, it is uncertain what this might achieve - beyond seriously embarrassing Ernest and exacerbating the troubled relationship with him. The Audit Committee might in future be less likely to trust Ernest, and could even press for a reprimand but not necessarily for his dismissal.

Hence, following any such disclosures, deterioration of working relationships for the audit could lead to the early loss of the appointment. Whilst this would be likely to bring adverse reputational and commercial repercussions for your firm and, hence, yourself, without a change by Ernest, there could be only limited expectations of improved conditions for another CA firm taking on the assignment.

Are there any other comments?

Is this situation acceptable as bringing the 'least bad' outcome within an imperfect systemic arrangement, where human relationships and weaknesses have also to be accommodated? However, is it acceptable for you as a CA that your employer has been, apparently, so accommodating to Ernest?

Would your ethical perspective be different if the amounts were significantly lower, or larger?

Scenario 2: The weekend expenses claim

You are the London-based senior manager responsible for an audit being undertaken for a 'public sector' client in Norfolk. The junior staff, normally London-based, have been working at the client's premises for three weeks, staying in a nearby hotel for the Monday to Thursday nights and returning for the weekends. They used, and have claimed for, rail travel. With your prior approval the 'auditor-in-charge', who had also been there for three weeks, drove to the assignment from London using her own car, carrying the files. On a daily basis, she transported the other staff members between hotel and client premises, thus avoiding the costs of more expensive taxis. Her car also brought the files back to London.

You now receive her expense claim form. This seeks re-imbursement at standard (HMRC approved) rates for the costs of the mileage she has actually undertaken. Appropriately, normal 'travel-to-work' deductions have been made. But in addition she has claimed for First Class return rail fares between Norfolk and London for each of the two weekends. This is marked as being 'rail fare in lieu of mileage', thereby roughly conforming to your firm's policy on expenses relating to client or firm's activities. This allows staff, at their own preference, to use a private car but to claim a train fare where higher costs of car mileage have not been given prior authorisation.

However, from having chatted socially with the 'in-charge', you know this claim has a fictitious element. She enjoyed the opportunity on both weekends to stay with her parents who live in Norfolk. You appreciate that the 'in charge' accountant left later than other staff on both Fridays. Moreover, you know from phone conversations that she had arrived back at the client's premises on Monday at 9.00 am, and so well ahead of those staff who had returned to London for the weekend. Thus, at least eight hours of otherwise 'travel time' was spent more productively on the client's behalf.

Nevertheless, you consider it an ethical concern that a qualified CA has submitted a monetary claim for journeys that both you and she know never took place. You ask your managers for their views on what you should now do. One argues that you should accept that the 'in-charge' has used her car and her weekend stays in Norfolk not only for her own convenience but to enhance the overall efficiency of the audit. There have been significant savings of both time and transport. You should recognise that she had an entitlement to travel back to London by train for the weekend. You should authorise the claim without comment, ignoring information from social chat.

Another, from a public sector background, argues, that the claim is blatantly 'false accounting'. You should reject the claim, pointing out that no CA should submit a claim for travel that he or she knows never took place. Only actual journeys can be reimbursed. Untaxed 'reimbursements' cannot properly be used to reward efficiency savings of travel time. As an example, the CA should be reported within the firm and expect disciplinary action both by the firm and ICAS, as her professional institute.

The third suggests that he will tell the 'in charge' to tell you that on both Saturdays, she had driven back to London to watch a football match. The rail fares were then 'in lieu'. You do not need to ask whether this is true. You can authorise her return fare with a clear conscience even though you know she strongly dislikes sports events.

What do you do now?

Scenario 2: Analysis

What are the readily-identifiable ethical issues for your decision?

For you personally

What action do you take and how do you explain your decision to the different parties?

For the CA firm

Can the 'false accounting' in such circumstances be compatible with professional obligations for integrity, so that 'fairness' appears to prevail over 'truth'?

Although the sums claimed may lack materiality in the context of the audit fee and related costs, they seem to matter to the 'in-charge'. Her co-operation has benefited the client and appears a 'win-win'. Can this/should this be 'rewarded' through an expenses system as being swift and simple?

Who are the key parties who can influence, or will be affected by, your decision?

'You' as the person responsible for authorising; the 'in-charge'; the three managers; and the firm's staff generally.

What fundamental ethical principles for accountants are most applicable and is there an apparent conflict between them?

Integrity	*Is the sense of 'wholeness' that is essential to integrity threatened by any instance where a CA makes a statement on a financial matter that is knowingly false?*
Objectivity	*Assumed*
Professional competence and due care	*Assumed*
Confidentiality	*Should you seek to compartmentalise information learned from staff in social conversation from specifically work-focused discussion?* *Would the 'in-charge' be justified in expecting that you would raise your concerns first with her rather than consulting about her actions with your fellow managers/her line managers?*
Professional behaviour	*Should the second suggestion, of a disciplinary action, be made to establish a point of principle?*

Is there any further information (including legal obligations) or discussion that might be relevant?

The firm's guidance is not specific for circumstances such as these - you have already checked!

Does the 'public sector' client have a travel policy that gives specific guidance on weekend arrangements? If so, this may be stricter than the firm's (or a commercial counterpart's) and might be applicable for this situation. However, this does not address the generic issues.

HMRC guidance on reimbursable expenses.

Is there a conflict between the 'Guardian' and 'Commercial' strands of an accountant's responsibilities?

Yes. A 'Commercial' approach would seek to minimise the bureaucratic element and detailed rules. It would also encourage efficiencies, savings and co-operative use of resources. But in this situation there is an inherent confusion. The claim for journeys not taken by the 'auditor-in-charge' shares between her and the client the savings from the co-operative use of her private resources - her car and access to her parent's home (coincidently nearby). Yet the amount she has claimed - of the foregone rail fare - while seeming pragmatic, is coincidental and illogical. It is not linked to what she has foregone (the weekends in her own flat). The travel costs of her journeys not undertaken are based on distance and have no correlation with weekend time, whether in London or at her parents (i.e. had the client and her stay been 500 miles away in, say, Inverness, she might have claimed a much bigger London–Inverness rail fare for the same foregone). Although using travel expenses to substitute for some form of reward system has the merits of providing a swift and accessible form of incentive/'compensation', it creates anomalies that could lead to loss of integrity.

A more 'Guardian-orientated' approach would ignore the efficiencies and see 'expenses' as only ever 're-imbursement of the costs actually incurred in delivering a stipulated service'. They cannot be some form of entitlement, reward or incentive. Allowing, perhaps sometimes even encouraging, expenses to be viewed as any of these three, could be detrimental as pushing the relatively junior CA towards the loss of her integrity.

Based on the information available, is there scope for an imaginative solution?

The first suggestion is the easiest but may perpetuate malpractice; the second (while principled) seems to discourage initiative and additional 'give and take' commitment.

The third suggestion, that compounds the fictitious nature of the claim with fictitious attendance at weekend football matches, provides seemingly the most effective compromise but is likely to be the most damaging of integrity by encouraging further explicit lying.

Probably, the firm needs to have in place some tariff, or flat-rate arrangement, formally agreed with HMRC, that recognises the saved cost of a staff member voluntarily staying away over weekends, where this clearly benefits a client.

Are there any other comments?

Expense claims came across as a pervasive problem in the discussions for preparing the scenarios. Perhaps they are rarely raised as a major ethical concern in that, individually, they cover relatively small sums. However, their frequently recurring nature, especially for more junior staff, could make them corrosive with progressive loss of integrity through small deceits. It may be for this reason that 'public service' bodies have a more rigorous approach. Perceived fairness, clarity and consistency in application seem important requirements. Their ubiquity makes them integral to the culture and the corporate conscience of any organisation.

Scenario 3: A student's insights

You are the junior partner in the medium-sized office of a medium-sized firm. You have recently assumed responsibility for Student Training. In this capacity you are reading over the self-assessment sections of the 'Achievement Logs' that ICAS students are required to maintain and submit. Students are specifically asked to reflect on and address areas of ethical concern. In one, you read the following account:

> *I was assigned to the audit of a long-standing client, a successful and profitable family company in the printing industry based in Scotland. As part of my work I was checking over the acquisition of fixed assets and found that capitalised items included an expensive and bespoke security system with sophisticated electronic detectors and metal shutters. Although invoices showed it charged to the company, it had been fitted at 'Newcourt Farmhouse' in rural South-West England. On enquiry, the financial controller told me that this is the newly acquired home of one of the Managing Director's adult children. For further details, I should speak with the Managing Director.*
>
> *With the agreement of the audit manager, I did so. He explained that the security system was part of a wedding gift from himself and his wife to one of their daughters. When I questioned further why this was paid for directly by the company and why it was included as its asset, he said that they hoped to be making visits to see grandchildren at some future date. He might take with him work-related documents so that having appropriate security would be necessary. He implied that, in his view the amounts were not material to the business or to his personal circumstances. He also said that the auditors had not questioned previous bookings to the company of both fixed assets and operational expenses relating to family-owned properties.*

I described his response to the firm's long-standing taxation manager. She expressed mild surprise but advised that the matter be brought to the attention of the engagement partner. My audit manager agreed to include in our formal internal audit clearance document a couple of paragraphs that I had written covering this. I was not at the internal clearance meeting but understand that the partner also expressed only mild surprise. He said that he would raise the matter himself. Later, when signing off the engagement, he added the note 'Discussed with Managing Director. This is a misunderstanding. Fuller, satisfactory explanation now given.

Neither the audit nor taxation managers have shown any inclination to enquire about this further. The company's accounts have been finalised with no adjustment to the capitalisation. I felt that I should be told what I misunderstood. So, some weeks later, I took the opportunity at the end of the clearance meeting for another client to ask the engagement partner about it. This time, he seemed more than mildly surprised at being asked, but told me he would get back to me.

A couple of days later I was summoned by his secretary. The partner said I was right to raise my concerns. What he had meant was that it was the Managing Director who had misunderstood what I wanted to know. However, I had misreported him. He added that the company are planning to take on more work in security printing - exam papers and the like - and have been recommended by their insurers to get proper protection for handling this paperwork. I acknowledged that I had not known this. But I then said that I did not see how this could explain the past company expenditure on family-owned properties that the Managing Director had referred to. At this point, the partner got noticeably angry. He asked me if I had any specific evidence that this had happened. I replied 'no' but added it had been my first year on this audit. He said that he too had no evidence either and that the job of an auditor is to be a watchdog not a bloodhound. Over the years he had come to trust the Managing Director as a competent, shrewd and successful businessman. He wished me good luck with my forthcoming exams and made clear that our discussion was over.

Somehow, I feel my concerns have not been answered. There seems to be an approach with this client that follows Stevenson's line that 'them that ask no questions isn't told a lie, so watch the wall my darling while the gentlemen go by'. I find it difficult to square this philosophy with ICAS lectures on ethics.

The engagement partner is the office senior partner. He has long experience in client handling and is respected throughout the firm as a pragmatic decision-maker. Superficially at least, he is an affable and approachable person but he can be dismissive and has a fierce temper if provoked. You know that he does not take kindly to what he has termed 'impertinent students who have no experience of real life and are often too smart for their own good'.

This Achievement Log will need to be sent to ICAS shortly.

What do you do now?

Scenario 3: Analysis

What are the readily-identifiable ethical issues for your decision?

For you personally

Can you, while retaining your integrity, ignore what the student has written?

If not, how, appropriately, do you ascertain the accuracy or otherwise of the student's account before raising this with the engagement partner?

Assuming that you accept the credibility of what the student has described, how do you handle this instance of internal 'whistleblowing' in a manner that is fair and effective for all parties?

For the CA firm

How does the firm establish and maintain appropriate procedures whereby concerns of this nature (whether of training or of ethics) can be addressed effectively before being brought up in an individual student's Achievement Log?

Who are the key parties who can influence, or will be affected by, your decision?

'You'; the student; the engagement/senior partner; other staff (qualified and non-qualified); and the client (family members as well as the Managing Director). Also, ICAS - in the promotion of student training and of professional ethics - and HMRC.

What fundamental ethical principles for accountants are most applicable and is there an apparent conflict between them?

Integrity	*Is there a dichotomy between expectations and claims of members and what the students perceive (correctly or otherwise) to be happening in practice?*
Objectivity	*Has the student with a 'fresh eye' identified that the audit manager, 'longstanding' taxation manager and engagement partner have allowed a less than rigorous acceptance of questionable practices?*
Professional competence and due care	*While assumed, the managers need to be encouraged to play a greater part than has been apparent in assisting the partner to come to decisions and communicating these, by themselves asking questions, and not leaving it to students.*
Confidentiality	*Students should respect employers' and clients' confidentialities in Achievement Logs. But the ethical principle of 'Confidentiality' should not be misused as a handy means to avoid confronting unethical conduct. Nor is it a cloak to restrict legitimate training and necessary development by ICAS and other reputable educators.*
Professional behaviour	*Has this been adequate? Perhaps the student requires the courtesy of a more thorough explanation, albeit this needs to fit with the simultaneous demands of a time-pressured commercial practice.* *Furthermore, has the engagement partner overly focused on maintaining a relationship with the client as a 'competent, shrewd and successful businessman' rather than on wider responsibilities?*

Is there any further information (including legal obligations) or discussion that might be relevant?

The technical point, as to whether or not the security system should be booked as a valid asset of the company, is peripheral to consideration of the broader ethical concerns. However, if the firm investigates and discovers past 'personal' expenditure inappropriately treated as being 'company', it will need to advise both client and HMRC of corrective action.

Is there a conflict between the 'Guardian' and 'Commercial' strands of an accountant's responsibilities?

The firm's 'Commercial' incentive is to build and maintain a co-operative working relationship with a successful business owner. However, its 'Guardian' function requires that it must not let this intrude on the duty to ensure that information relating to the company (and on which shareholders and HMRC rely) is complete and accurate.

Based on the information available, is there scope for an imaginative solution?

Assuming that the student's account is credible, you need to persuade the senior partner that fuller explanations need to be sought and fuller explanations be given to staff. Requirements such as the ICAS Achievement Log may, indirectly, assist with this.

Are there any other comments?

You have a duty, perhaps particularly as student training partner, but also as a CA and as a partner, to ensure that the student is respected and will not be victimised for her diligence and courage in pursuing this matter. This may not be easy, but a necessary part of being a professional requires fortitude in sustaining professional standards.

Scenario 4: Temptation at the tender

Your target list of prospective audit clients has been in tatters recently. You have put together carefully constructed proposals only to be told, all too often, that your firm had been in 'second place'. Worse still, you have seen several client losses that have not been replaced. As a partner in an international firm where you have a fairly narrow audit speciality in financial services this is not good news - especially as, following a recent merger, rumours are swirling of a looming partner shake-out.

Six weeks ago, the Audit Committee of a medium-sized financial institution put its external audit out to tender. It followed the recent appointment of Cameron, as the new Finance Director (FD). Being two years earlier than the current auditors might have expected, there seemed good prospects of change. As invited, you and three other firms submitted proposals.

You had expected one of the firms would appear a winner at this stage. However, you were formally advised five days ago that both your firm and the current auditors had appeared similarly capable in terms of UK and international service quality and that the Audit Committee had had difficulty deciding. It has, therefore, now invited you and your competitor to refine your original submissions and to make a final presentational pitch. You will be delivering this tomorrow afternoon.

At a short interview with Cameron, he hinted that the tenders were different on price and that this will now be an influential factor. However, he gave you no clue as to whether your firm was the higher or lower. But, since then, you and your team have devoted much further time and energy to refine your proposal, carefully re-visiting each aspect of your audit planning but not finding much scope for change. Other partners have been very helpful with advice and support but you know that it is now you who has to make any final decisions and you who will need to give the convincing presentation. You have difficulty acknowledging, even to yourself, just how important it is that you win this client, in terms of boosting morale and lifting your flagging reputation, both within and outside the firm.

It is 7.00 pm. You have just finished a long call to the managing partner of the office where the prospective client has its present US subsidiary. It has openly referred to looking for US acquisitions and he is very keen indeed that your firm win this audit. He has re-iterated a willingness to be very flexible on sharing costs, support and fees between the national firms.

But first you have to win. Mulling over the US pricing discussion, you have begun rechecking the presentation slides when Fiona rushes in. Fiona has become a key member of your team, seconded from the firm's marketing department to support your bid. She tells you that, while you were on the phone, she took a brief call from Trevor, the Chief Internal Auditor at the prospective client. Trevor will almost certainly be attending in an advisory capacity tomorrow. He wants you to phone back, urgently. You do so, putting the call on loudspeaker.

Names confirmed and pleasantries over, Trevor comes quickly to the point:

> *Hope you are well set up for tomorrow. I want your firm to be appointed. You said all the right things last time. There needs to be a much more co-operative relationship between the Internal and External Auditors. I am not sure I can face another five years of the current auditors' carping about our methodologies. However, I thought that I should warn you that at their presentation this afternoon, they have really cut back their fees to keep the audit. Everywhere is sharper but their US pricing is particularly aggressive. Even Cameron, who prompted the tender and was for you last time, is now swithering!*
>
> *You should have won it outright last time, if the CEO hadn't persuaded the Chair to give the current auditors a second chance.*

It was really quite shameless. There's been a lot of politics going on. I am pretty sure too that your first round proposal was leaked. This place has a deserved reputation as a sieve.

I have your fax number. To even things up, I'll send over a hard copy of their slides now. That will give you all of their key pricing data. You can then decide how to play things to your best advantage - just don't say I have done so because I'll completely deny it of course! All is fair in 'Love' and 'War'.

If you have any really vital questions, you can get back to me on my mobile - it was in the scoping pack. Otherwise, forget this conversation. Good luck!

While you are digesting this information sufficient to give a coherent reply, Trevor has rung off. You turn to Fiona who looks startled but is smiling broadly. She leaves the office, saying:

Amazing! I'll go over to the fax machine and wait for it. There will just be time to do the adjustments tomorrow. This looks like it will be a real classic win for the firm and you richly deserve it! Your audit team will be mightily relieved too; they're all worried about their jobs!

This gives you time to think. You don't know Trevor very well, though he was an alumnus of your firm a decade ago. As part of your potential client targeting you have spoken to him socially a number of times. He has come across as mildly eccentric and having a determinedly independent streak - as well befits his Internal Audit role. During the scoping sessions for preparing the tenders he had been helpful but had made no reference to the apparent animosity between Internal Audit and the current external auditors. You had known that, years ago, the CEO had been an actuarial consultant with the current auditors. Now aware of Cameron's preference towards your own firm, you are trying to work out if his hint over fees was specific advice and so more than just a general ploy to encourage lower bids by both firms.

Fiona comes in with the fax of your competitor's presentation.

What do you do now?

Scenario 4: Analysis

What are the readily-identifiable ethical issues for your decision?

For you personally

If you take advantage of the privileged information that is being leaked covertly to you (i.e. you do not tell Fiona to take it away unread), will you have been compromised in your ability to conduct an external audit by having received it?

If you decide you should first consult with fellow partners, will you recommend that:

- *You read the fax, then adjust any parts of your proposal to be competitive on fees, and present tomorrow?*
- *You do not read the fax but look at the proposed fees only to take account of the willingness of your US firm to adjust and present tomorrow (without telling the prospective client of Trevor's phone call/fax)?*
- *You (first thing tomorrow) contact the prospective client's Chair about Trevor's phone call/fax?*
- *You report Trevor to his professional body's disciplinary committee?*

Whatever you decide, how do you discuss with Fiona her assumption that there are no ethical constraints to you and your firm, seeing this as a 'classic win'?

Whatever you decide, how do you address with 'your audit team' their worries about their jobs?

For the CA firm

How do prepare, guide and support partners and staff in competitive circumstances such as these?

Who are the key parties who can influence, or will be affected by, your decision?

'You'; your fellow partners; Fiona; your audit team; Trevor; the Audit Committee; Cameron; the CEO; and the current auditors as fellow professionals/competitors.

What fundamental ethical principles for accountants are most applicable and is there an apparent conflict between them?

Integrity	*There are clearly major pressures and incentives from self-interest for you to have access to the information in the fax but would it be 'fair dealing' for you to do so?*
Objectivity	*In the short-term, there are the significant temptations you must ignore to ensure objectivity (i.e. Trevor's speculation that your own proposal had been leaked to the other firm). Longer-term, if you win on the basis of the faxed data, could you have an objective, independent relationship with this client?*
Professional competence and due care	*Assumed*
Confidentiality	*Is it respectful of the other auditor firm to accept their confidential proposal details?*
Professional behaviour	*Does it serve the public interest to have the tender process distorted, or is it only one of several possible, but imperfect, mechanisms?*

Is there any further information (including legal obligations) or discussion that might be relevant?

Trevor's claim, that lying would be acceptable and 'fair' because the process of auditor selection is akin to 'Love and War', reflects an adversarial view of professional conduct and professional responsibilities that needs to be questioned.

Is there a conflict between the 'Guardian' and 'Commercial' strands of an accountant's responsibilities?

While seeking efficiency allows for research and enquiry to make a tender offer as 'commercially' competitive as is possible, boundaries are necessary. The 'Guardian' function of auditing requires that appropriate quality, not price, should be the overall determining factor. With 'Trust' integral to the audit role, there could, in future, be very significant complications if your relationship with the Internal Audit function is based on fear over wider disclosure of a past favour, received in secret.

The full implications of these factors may not have been appreciated by Fiona, given her different professional background from accountancy and solely 'commercial' background.

Based on the information available, is there scope for an imaginative solution?

You need to consult with other partners. Meanwhile, you could phone Trevor, to tell him that you have decided not to read the fax. You inform Fiona also that this is your decision. You note that you must have a frank discussion with your staff about prospects once the outcome of this tender is known. You then discuss with fellow partners how to proceed with regards to informing other parties.

Are there any other comments?

The temptation could be that you do all of the steps described under the 'imaginative solution' but only after covertly reading the fax. For Fiona, you could attribute any late changes you might make to reduce the bottom-line of the prospective fees to your following of the advice from the US. In this way, you would present yourself discreetly but publicly as having acted in a manner respectful of high ethical standards but still have benefited (secretly) from the inside information. The fax might merely have confirmed that your prospective fees were already lower. You would not press the issues in relation to reporting Trevor or of future working with him, on the grounds that you had acted swiftly to close down the leak. While clearly completely lacking in 'integrity', is there a risk you could persuade yourself that this constitutes suitable 'professional behaviour' in that you have appeared to uphold this principle, and you alone know otherwise? The ethical essentials of 'conscience' and 'self-discipline' are discussed on pages 197 to 198.

This scenario conveys something of the competitive pressures upon an individual to accept the proffered information when feeling lonely and vulnerable (rather than, say, motivated solely by monetary reward). It could be tempting too to justify reading the fax as little different from networking and intelligence-gathering about business contacts. 'Loneliness' when making decisions, even within a many-partnered firm, was a recurring theme within the research behind the case studies. This emphasises the importance of consulting colleagues over ethical concerns. This will also be covered in chapter five, the conclusion sections of the report.

The situation outlined in this scenario could arise in many different industries. An extended variant, set in banking and with 'Trevor' offering the information in return for a donation to a favoured charity, was analysed at greater length in a 2004 article in the journal, 'Business Ethics: a European Review' by David Molyneaux, with Lucia Webster and David Kennedy.

Scenario 5: Partnership problems

You are the junior partner in a successful three-partner practice. It is the summer holiday season. Your mid-ranking colleague, Bernard, left last week for four weeks of trekking in Mongolia as part of a long-planned celebration of a special anniversary. Newly back from a rare fortnight's break is the workaholic senior partner and founder of the practice, Alex.

On his return, Alex and yourself had hosted a restaurant lunch party to mark the successful exam results of two of your students. Alex, who traditionally deals with all aspects of the partnership finances, had paid, using the partnership's credit card. You had noted this because Alex had got up to settle at the desk and seemed disconcerted by the PIN machine being brought to the table. He had laughed it off with a typical bad pun, that he was making 'rather a meal of it'. Moreover, in banter with the waitress he had referred to what had seemed to you to be a remarkably large sum that he was adding as a gratuity.

Next day you learned that, overnight, Alex had been taken to the Emergency Care unit of the local hospital, following a serious heart attack. You took on the tasks of dealing with mail, finance etc that would normally have been dealt with exclusively by Alex, or in his absence, by Bernard.

Among the items passed to you for signature was a cheque together with an expense claim form, prepared and authorised by Alex on the afternoon before he was taken ill. It was for re-imbursement to himself of the cost of the celebratory lunch. The detailed supporting bill was attached with gratuity added. Given your recollection that payment was by the partnership credit card, this greatly surprised you but you were too busy to investigate immediately. Meanwhile, you arranged for Alex's cheque to be banked.

However, your curiosity was seriously aroused when, three days later, with Alex in Intensive Care, you opened the envelope with the statements for the partnership credit card. As usual there were three statements, one for each of the three cardholders that set out only the purchases made by each respective cardholder. Normally, you get only your own statement for you to review, annotate and return to Alex. This time, you look at Alex's statement. Not only was the last item the restaurant bill for which he had made a claim but there were three items amounting to £720 that appeared to be for Alex's private purchases, such as for car hire in California where he had taken his recent holiday.

This seems in complete breach of your own understanding and usage of the card, that it should relate only to direct partnership purchases. You looked at Bernard's statement but there seemed nothing unusual in it.

You asked the bookkeeper (who has been loyally with the firm for many years) about arrangements for settlement of the credit card total. She explained that this is automatic. For years, it has been paid in full each month by direct debit. She does not herself see the detailed statements. For her records, Alex gives her a slip with the total as supplied by the credit card company. You asked her if the balance was ever amended for personal transactions and she expressed surprise at the question. From this you deduced that it was not. You asked if she knows the whereabouts of the detailed statements and she explained that Alex has traditionally kept these at home.

However, she could and did give you the expense claim forms for the period covered by the one detailed credit card statement for Alex that you do have. Apart from the recent restaurant bill, you found one other practice-related duplication. This was from just before Alex's holiday. He had claimed directly for a meal with a client that was also charged to the card. You noticed, ruefully, that here too the gratuity seemed very generous but realise that it would suit a double claimant to maximise the bill.

You contacted the credit card company. They responded that they will only supply duplicates of past statements if required by the Police or by an authorisation letter from at least two of the partners. Meanwhile, Alex's recovery has been slow. You know Bernard will be away for at least another fortnight.

However, Alex, now in a high dependency ward, has apparently been pressing to see you. Yesterday, with much reluctance, Alex's wife agreed to this. Amid tears she explained that the doctors consider that Alex's recovery will be protracted. She told you, in confidence, of her fears that undue stress could trigger in Alex a recurrence of a psychiatric disorder he had experienced a decade or so before. You had not previously known of this condition.

Five minutes ago, when you entered the ward you could see that Alex was clearly still far from well. Immediately on seeing you, he became agitated, seemingly sensing that you had discovered something suspicious. Ignoring pleasantries, he started out by telling you that he had been under a great amount of stress of late and that he is now very concerned that there may have been a few confusions within partnership financial matters. He went on to say that he would be able readily to sort matters out as soon as he is fit to do so. He has just asked you to promise that you will not discuss partnership matters with anyone else, including Bernard, until he, Alex, has had the opportunity to check over things himself.

You are thinking over how to reply when you see a senior nurse hurrying towards you. You realise that Alex's agitation has set off a monitoring alarm and she will probably ask you to leave the ward forthwith.

What do you do now?

Scenario 5: Analysis

What are the readily-identifiable ethical issues for your decision?

For you personally

Should you accede to Alex's immediate wish, on an expediency basis, in order to help calm his concerns?

If you accede (and in that no one else knows of your suspicions) how long do you allow Alex for recovery before you discuss your evidence/suspicions with Bernard? Should you tell Bernard directly on his return?

Should you contact the firm's regulators? If so, when? For example: should you wait until Bernard's return? This might be justifiable in order first to obtain authorisation of the further information from the credit card company and so determine if the duplications/personal charges have been a temporary lapse, or extended malpractice, but will there then be other reasons for delay? While it is very likely you will need legal advice, how much will your decisions be influenced by legal or ethical considerations, including those for Alex's health?

For the CA firm

How will the interests of clients and of staff be sustained during this period of turmoil for the firm's partners?

Who are the key parties who can influence, or will be affected by, your decision?

'You', Alex; Alex's wife (who may or may not know); Bernard; the practice's clients and staff; regulators and HMRC.

What fundamental ethical principles for accountants are most applicable and is there an apparent conflict between them?

Integrity	*While it is in your self-interest (as a possible victim of theft) to have the situation investigated and misappropriations/duplications quantified promptly, how much consideration should you give to Alex's health situation?* *As a (part) owner of the accountancy practice, it may be in your commercial interest to do and say nothing further, but would this be consistent with fair dealing and truthfulness?*
Objectivity	*Given the other ongoing demands upon you (with two of the three fellow partners away), how can you ensure that you approach this matter in an entirely focused way?*
Professional competence and due care	*Assumed, although given the likely demands of this issue, how will you maintain your concentration on your clients' affairs over a sustained period?*
Confidentiality	*While it is in the interests of all parties that any process of investigation be kept confidential until suspicions are confirmed or explained, how long should this be delayed by the exigencies of Alex's uncertain health?*
Professional behaviour	*Although disclosure may be damaging to the practice, the interests of clients and the wider public have to be recognised.*

Is there any further information (including legal obligations) or discussion that might be relevant?

You have a professional obligation to report suspicions of malpractice by other members to their Institute. There could be taxation consequences for the partnership's past returns.

Is there a conflict between the 'Guardian' and 'Commercial' strands of an accountant's responsibilities?

As a partner, your 'Commercial' interests are likely to be best served by minimal publicity, possibly leaving any investigation until after Alex has returned. From a 'Guardian' perspective, any malpractice needs to be exposed and corrected promptly.

Based on the information available, is there scope for an imaginative solution?

None obvious.

Are there any other comments?

Such situations, even when less dramatic than that described, are profoundly difficult for all involved but are unlikely to benefit anyone through delay in seeking authoritative support.

Scenario 6: The disaster waiting to happen!

It is 11 am on a Monday morning. You are the partner with responsibility for ethics in a medium-sized firm. Charles, your fellow (but more senior) partner has interrupted one of your own client meetings for an urgent consultation. He wants immediate advice regarding his prestigious client, McAverty Agricultural and Estate Holdings Limited ['MAEHL']. This is the holding company for the disparate land and agricultural activities of Sir Alasdair and Lady McAverty.

Your firm has been financial and tax adviser to the family for generations, hence you already have some familiarity with the client. Succinctly, Charles briefs you as to more recent developments. Having been MAEHL's auditor for decades until the audit threshold was raised, thereafter, the firm has continued to provide an accountancy service. This includes collating the quarterly management accounts from information supplied by the company. Under an arrangement set up by a former partner, Charles reviews these with MAEHL's two directors, Sir Alasdair and the Estate Factor, prior to their submission to the bank and various other parties.

Since inheriting MAEHL sixteen years ago, Sir Alasdair has been energetic in his diversification and investment in 'modern' organic beef and poultry rearing as well as the growing of quality wheat and barley and various other estate activities including clay-pigeon shooting and a golf range. The ambitious capital programme has been funded through a mixture of grants, sales of surplus land for housing development and the receipt of a substantial 'dowry' from a trust set up by the parents of Lady McAverty - Belinda to her friends. Belinda herself has shown minimal interest in farming or business although her father, an eminent banker, now retired and in his 70's, continues to be quoted in the financial press for his strong views on a number of financial and political subjects.

Operationally, MAEHL has depended on bank lending, secured against the land and beautiful Georgian farmhouse that the family occupy. Although the operations have been very well run and resources deployed shrewdly, interest payments on the bank borrowings have been a constant drain on profitability. So too have been Sir Alasdair's salary and dividend payments, required to fund a certain life-style - five children in private education; expensive skiing holidays and travel; ponies and domestic staff - required 'to keep Belinda happy' as Sir Alasdair puts it.

Over the past five years that he has been engagement partner, Charles believes that he has established a good working relationship of mutual respect with Sir Alasdair. They now golf and shoot together but beyond this, Charles credits Sir Alasdair with having re-vitalised his family's assets; become overseer of a decisive and cannily-run business enterprise and as being a person ready to embrace new ideas. These included, from the start of the investment programme, selling forward all the different agricultural products to ensure predictability and stability. This practice has generally been seen as a success, particularly by the bank.

However, four years ago, Sir Alasdair, apparently confident in his knowledge as 'a real farmer' and so able to spot market trends, had started MAEHL trading in more complex wheat futures. Using the facilities of MAEHL's existing brokers, this went beyond the forward sale of its own physical crops. The sums involved had been modest, as had the small loss thereby generated. Because of its immateriality, this had not been separately identified in the management accounts, statutory accounts or tax returns but absorbed within the records of 'forward sales'. There had been the same treatment in the following year, when there had been a small profit. Charles recalled that at their quarterly meetings, Sir Alasdair had referred to these transactions only in passing. Details had been sidelined in the discussion of other matters, including the many wider difficulties that, despite constantly improving productivity, the farming enterprise was encountering.

Last year, Sir Alasdair had talked a little more about the 'futures'. He was pleased that they had generated a year-end outcome of

£70,000 profit. Amid gloom at negative outflows elsewhere, this had enabled him to upgrade some essential farm machinery and provided the deposit on a new Range Rover 4x4 and horsebox. At that point of the meeting, Charles had been reluctant to interrupt Sir Alasdair's enthusiastic description of his daughters' show-jumping successes with specific enquiries as to whether the bank, Belinda or the other parties receiving MAEHL's financial information were aware as to the source of this new money.

Three days ago, at the review of the latest quarterly management accounts, there had been no reference made to 'futures' trading in the current year. Instead, Charles had pointed out that while the overdraft was currently at a seasonal low, it was at a level £400,000 higher than three years ago. This was despite sales of almost all of the surplus property. Charles felt he had been helpfully forthright in stressing that, while the peak overdraft projections would still be just within the security levels sought by the bank, MAEHL was now so seriously indebted it had very limited room for future manoeuvre. Both Sir Alasdair and the Estate Factor had reacted calmly to this and seemed fully aware of the funding problem.

However, later that day, Friday, on the pretext of discussing another matter but significantly without the Estate Factor present, Sir Alasdair had casually mentioned that unless markets changed, MAEHL would have potential losses on wheat futures of '£500,000 beyond the losses in the management accounts'. Shocked, Charles had listened while Alasdair explained how, opportunistically, a few weeks ago, he had entered MAEHL into various short-term futures trades, hoping substantially to reduce the overdraft. Instead, the market had moved dramatically against him. However, so sure is he that the specialist commodity futures market is out of touch with actual harvest conditions, that he will be using the low point of the overdraft borrowing cycle in order to 'invest' the spare £400,000 overdraft capacity in separate 'counter-measures'. Time is quite short for recovery but this will involve transactions in physical crops that he will plan to deliver independently of whatever happens with the futures market. By this means, and ahead of the year-end, he expects to have offset the contingent losses. However, he also hopes that there might also be substantial gains as the futures market erratically 're-adjusts' to what, with his expert knowledge, he insists will become 'the true market position'.

Alarmed at this news and his attitude, Charles had, for the first time, asked whether the bank, the Estate Factor or Belinda knew of the existence, let alone the scale, of the more complex futures activities (as opposed to the forward trading). Sir Alasdair had responded fiercely that he had seen no point in discussing it with them when it was small and, equally, he saw no point in doing so now, since he is certain that his additional investment in 'counter-measures' will provide a solution. Charles had urged that Sir Alasdair should tell all three parties immediately. But he admits to you that he had not pressed very hard when Sir Alasdair had brusquely rejected 'asking someone else's permission' for how to use MAEHL's authorised overdraft facility.

Yesterday, Sunday, Charles had met Belinda at church. She had taken him aside and said she was sure that there was something wrong with her husband recently - he had even been fretful after a day's fishing - and she wanted to know if it was to do with a mistress, or with business. Charles admitted that he had felt less than convincing in trying to explain that they were not at an appropriate venue to discuss such matters. Belinda had then ended the conversation:

> *All right, Charles, I appreciate you cannot answer if Alasdair is keeping some 'tart'. But if this is really just about money, as you know, my parents and I have always relied on you to keep an eye on Alasdair and what he is up to with MAEHL. If he won't tell me, then I expect to get the facts from you. If you don't tell me, then we shall assume that business is not the problem.*

The reference to Belinda's father had prompted Charles, first thing this morning, to go back in the firm's files to look at correspondence from fifteen years ago. Letters had covered the terms under which Belinda's family trust had provided funds - by way of non-interest charging loans - to MAEHL, including limits on the activities in which it could engage. Like MAEHL's Articles of Association, these had been relatively tightly drawn and, while permitting forward selling, quite probably did not allow 'futures trading'. The terms had also stipulated the submission of quarterly management accounts, without being precise as to their detail or status. This had been the origins of your firm's contract to collate these and the trust had been sent these ever since. Although there had been subsequent, updated letters of engagement, these had been relatively vague about respective responsibilities.

An hour or so ago, Charles had phoned Sir Alasdair telling him of his conversation with Belinda - although only indirectly mentioning the suggestion of a mistress - and urging that Sir Alasdair discuss the monetary situation with her. He had flatly refused. He had also flatly refused to raise the matter with the bank ahead of implementing his intended plan to use the 'spare' overdraft facility to buy physical crops. Instead, he had re-iterated his intention to press ahead with entering into contractual obligations, this afternoon.

Charles had phoned MAEHL's lawyers (who also act for 'your' firm) for advice. The partner to whom he most wants to speak is in court all day. Charles, admitting that he is now in something of a panic, wants your urgent advice, as ethics partner, as to what he should do before Sir Alasdair starts his 'counter-measures' program. This, he fears, will compound, not offset, the contingent losses from the futures trading.

What do you do now?

Scenario 6: Analysis

What are the readily-identifiable ethical issues for your decision?

For you personally

How do you advise Charles? Is it ethical for him to breach confidentiality obligations/expectations of Sir Alasdair (as a director of MAEHL) in order to alert timeously some, or all, of Belinda, the Trustees, the Bank and the Estate Factor (as a director of MAEHL) to the further excessive financial risks being planned and recognising the potentially serious implications for each of these parties?

How do you advise Charles to address the complications that may arise from your firm's past failure to report to the Trust over the, quite probably, unauthorised futures trading?

How do you, as ethics partner, prioritise this matter over your own client meeting?

For the CA firm

How are partners trained and prepared to be able to make ethical decisions where speed may be essential?

Who are the key parties who can influence, or will be affected by, your decision?

'You'; Charles; Sir Alasdair; Belinda and the family; The Trust/trustees/ Belinda's father; the Bank; the Factor; MAEHL's brokers; the counter parties to the proposed physical purchases; and your own client (interrupted in mid-meeting).

What fundamental ethical principles for accountants are most applicable and is there an apparent conflict between them?

Integrity	*Respecting Belinda's; the Trust's (and the bank's (?)) reasonable expectations of your firm's role in relation to MAEHL even if this has not been formally expressed*
Objectivity	*Charles has come to you in a state of some panic, for a second opinion - how do you do give it constructively, frankly and fairly, without (at this stage) implying criticism as to how the situation has arisen?* *How can the issue of whether or not futures trading was 'ultra vires' (and so with possible implications in terms of your firm's letters of engagement and reporting to the Trust) avoid complicating decisions on the current situation?*
Professional competence and due care	*Not directly applicable for you personally. For Charles there may have been a past failure through excess deference or over-familiarity. How is this now to be remedied?*
Confidentiality	*Are you justified in recommending to Charles that, in the circumstances, he break expected confidentialities? Ethically, is he entitled to try to minimise the impact of a client's apparent wilfulness in implementing a highly risky strategy without proper consultation with other parties who have considerable vested interests in the potential consequences?*
Professional behaviour	*As designated ethics partner, how do you reconcile the competing conflicts of interest in a manner that can be respected by all parties?*

Is there any further information (including legal obligations) or discussion that might be relevant?

Ascertaining if the Bank has imposed restrictions on the use of overdraft facilities so that its staff must be consulted prior to the implementation of Sir Alasdair's plan. However, in that he intends to purchase physical crops (albeit on a speculative basis), the situation may be less clear than over the use of funds for futures trading.

Is there a conflict between the 'Guardian' and 'Commercial' strands of an accountant's responsibilities?

Not an obvious conflict in this immediate situation. 'Guardian' and 'Commercial' interests appear broadly aligned - to prevent inappropriate and damaging use of funds at a client. Ironically, the dilemma may have arisen through Sir Alasdair attempting to apply traditional 'Guardian' approaches and values to 'Commercial' opportunities without fully understanding the consequences. Charles, so far, has appeased rather than challenged, perhaps also having been confused as to his role.

Longer-term, there are issues to be explored over the need to respect boundaries on 'Confidentiality' for the preservation both of good order ('Guardian') and of trust ('Commerce').

Based on the information available, is there scope for an imaginative solution?

Not obvious, but urgent consultation with the Estate Factor, who as a director is entitled to be informed - where Belinda is not (deliberately?) - might point to a solution.

It might be possible to urge Sir Alasdair to delay the 'counter-measures' while MAEHL's lawyers determine if any of the futures trading has been 'ultra vires', in terms of the Articles of Association, and hence can be annulled - although this is primarily a legal solution and may give rise to various disputes with the Brokers who have acted in good faith.

Are there any other comments?

The need to deal with autocratic personalities, loose controls and their excess consumption of corporate resources/cover-up could arise in many guises and with varied reasons for their assumed authority and status.

Scenario 7: When cash is king

You are a recently qualified CA (with the proverbial spouse, mortgage and two small children) who has just taken up your first, well-paid post in industry as the Financial Controller and Company Secretary for a well-established family business.

This is a supplier of equipment and parts to photographers. It operates both a mail order and a warehouse-style operation in a large urban catchment area. There is a large customer base that ranges through enthusiastic amateurs, part-time and semi-professional photographers to bigger-scale, full-time studio operators that produce health and safety films and promotional clips. Payment methods reflect this diversity with some credit card transactions; many customers with 30-day credit business accounts and a surprisingly large number who collect the goods and pay by cash. On asking, you are told that this latter preference probably reflects the nature of their own receipts, such as for one-off wedding and weekend work that may have been paid for in cash.

On the Tuesday of your first week, the Sales Director (the principal shareholder's son) brings into your office a cheque in settlement of the monthly account of a major customer, whose representative you can see waiting in his office. The Sales Director explains that the cheque is for 10% more than the amount actually due. This is because the sales ledger balance excludes the bulk discount calculated retrospectively when monthly purchases exceed a pre-agreed amount. The Sales Director shows you on the customer file both the calculation and the board's on-going authorisation of a monthly bulk discount to this studio business.

Briefly, he explains that this situation arises most months. As usual, the studio's managing director has come to collect the discount in cash. 'Cash-back' on cheques is an option offered to only relatively few, larger customers as selected and agreed by the board. To those that take it up, it seems an important part of co-operative and friendly relationships that helps sustain the loyalty of their purchasing. The company keeps a substantial 'float' from its cash takings specifically for this purpose.

The Sales Director comments that the arrangement has the significant merit that thereby he secures a regular face-to-face meeting with the senior staff of major customers. Moreover, your predecessor has commented that it avoids the high charges that banks levy for taking cash, whereas the single cheque (which would need to be banked anyway) reduces the cash handling.

You ask why these customer representatives want cash rather than, more simply, their mailing in a cheque for the net amount. The Sales Director gives a wink and replies, '*Well that's their business isn't it?*' On this occasion you do as asked, but start to question, can you, should you accept this practice?

On the Wednesday, you start to try to understand the seemingly complex arrangements for different discounts and terms, both received from suppliers and, particularly, those offered to customers. Fortunately, the small team of sales assistants appear well versed in the requirements, all being of long-standing and committed to the business. One of them tells you that there is a pool of business account customers who are regular but not large-scale purchasers. As an incentive, they have been offered 'loyalty' cards and a type of account that states that it gives them an automatic discount of 15%. What is less clear is which of the several different pricelists the 15% is calculated against. The computerised billing processes have a small software program whereby the base price for purchases by these specified customers can be automatically lifted to the most expensive price. This practice has been in operation for some years and is known to staff as 'the Violin' - or 'fiddle'!

The transaction documentation given, or sent, to the customer is always mathematically correct. The sales assistant agrees that it is surprising but, seemingly, very few of these customers, when they receive their equipment or account, check the details of their bills, beyond that they have received the 15% discount. Where there has been the occasional challenge, the Sales Director has offered excuses; made a profuse apology;

offered an additional recompense (usually a piece of free equipment) and also, thereafter, discontinued the automatic uplift for that particular customer (while retaining the 15% discount). The same complaint from the same customer has never recurred and no one in the customer base seems aware of 'the Violin'.

When you question the Sales Director about these arrangements, he explains that his periodic calculations show that the value of the additional margin obtained through 'the Violin' is significant; the terminology used to promote the 15% is sufficiently ambiguous that it cannot be legally challenged and that the great majority of customers using this card/account seem satisfied with the net prices that they pay. Uncomfortable with what you have heard, you wonder, whether you should probe further about this policy.

On the Friday, the Managing Director (who is also the founder and principal shareholder) comes to your office and asks you to give him £525 in cash from the safe. He hands you, as if by way of receipt, a journal voucher showing his authorisation to write off parts/equipment for a similar amount. He explains:

It matches a couple of items that went out of stock when we sold them this morning. I have described them as 'damaged in a warehouse accident'. The transaction was for cash so I have voided the invoice. I run a tight ship here. Only I, as Managing Director, can authorise these slips and I don't do it very often. Quite rightly, your predecessor insisted that when I do, I must deal with the documentation immediately to keep the book-keeping right.

Receiving cash is part of our business and banking it is an expensive hassle. If family or senior staff members, such as yourself, want cash, that's fine by me, provided of course that they give you a matching cheque! I only want to know if a cheque bounces. Only one person has ever done that to me. He'll never do it again!

Unprepared for this, you do as asked, but feel very uncomfortable about it. Shortly afterwards, you decide that you cannot accept this practice and you'll use the week-end to think over how to raise the matter most effectively with the Managing Director.

So, at the end of your first week, you are about to return home to your flat. This is in a large, divided Victorian house, shared with four other owner-occupiers. Some months before, all residents had agreed on the need to deal urgently with an outbreak of dry rot and to put in place various roof repairs. One neighbour (from the top floor!) had agreed to organise this and had obtained three quotes. Two were more expensive and indicated long delays before work could start. The third quote (coming through a personal contact) was lower, had no VAT added and the work could start promptly. You and your neighbours had all agreed on the latter.

The works have been completed satisfactorily, using a team that came in the early evenings and weekends - an arrangement that the flat owners had found suited their need to give access to their properties. The team seemed a well-established business, properly equipped and efficiently organised.

The neighbour had asked you last weekend for payment of £2,500 that the contractor wants to receive in cash and for which he will not be giving receipts. Your other neighbours have all already settled up in cash. You need to deal with this matter, if not this weekend, at least early next week. Being so busy with the new job, you had forgotten about it. You have the money in your bank account but you have been reluctant to go to the branch to draw out such a large sum in cash. Although entirely legal, it would be a most unusual transaction on your account as you normally pay using credit or debit cards, or cheque. Daily use of an ATM would be impractical. You had decided to insist on paying by cheque. But it occurs to you that drawing from the business' cash float - in return, of course, for your completely matching personal cheque - could be an imaginative means of getting this particular problem off your plate.

What do you do now?

Scenario 7: Analysis

What are the readily-identifiable ethical issues for your decision?

For you personally

The Managing Director's 'take' of £525 in cash, even if occasional, is clearly contrary to acceptable accountancy standards as 'false accounting'. So, without succumbing to the threats of 'self-interest' and 'intimidation', how do 'you' explain this to the Managing Director?

Can/should the Financial Controller recommend to the Board the ending of the 'cash-back' scheme, where a bulk discount is genuinely given and the repayment in cash is a cheaper alternative to a cheque? Is the risk, that customers may misuse the opportunity to misrepresent costs in their own financial returns to HMRC, a compelling reason for its discontinuance?

The 'pseudo-discount' of the loyalty scheme seems a scam on customers but how much is it the responsibility of the Financial Controller/Company Secretary to question this, when the Sales Director asserts that it is not illegal?

Is it reportable suspicion, or speculation, that the contractor seeking cash for work on your flat will misrepresent to HMRC over income?

The personal situation and request for cash highlights whether there could be a loss of integrity between personal conduct and in an official capacity? Should there be any differentiation between your attitude to cash at your employment and in your personal financial arrangements?

Is it appropriate to start using the company's cash float - as suggested by the Managing Director - for your own convenience?

Who are the key parties who can influence, or will be affected by, your decision?

'You'; the Managing Director; the Sales Director; customers; minority shareholders; the business' auditors/financial advisers (depending on size); your neighbours; the contractor; HMRC.

What fundamental ethical principles for accountants are most applicable and is there an apparent conflict between them?

Integrity	*Should you seek to impose standards expected of you as a professional accountant onto more senior non-accountants (e.g. the Sales Director or the Managing Director) in the same business venture? Can a distinction be drawn between 'officer' and 'personal' so that the fundamental ethical principles apply to your professional and business relationships but do not extend also to your personal dealings?*
Objectivity	*How can you overcome the threats of 'self interest' and potential 'intimidation' sufficiently to retain the post, if only in order to establish and maintain more acceptable professional standards?*
Professional competence and due care	*Assumed, other than that deliberately and knowingly facilitating/accepting a false record of a transaction (as requested by the Managing Director) falls below required technical and professional standards. The significant test of professional skills will come with communicating this point to the Managing Director and persuading him of the need to reverse the erroneous journal entry and to change practices in future.*
Confidentiality	*Should you look for an early discussion with the company's auditor/financial adviser? What disclosures will be necessary over (apparently) past abuses?*
Professional behaviour	*The Financial Controller has an unavoidable responsibility in relation to all the company's financial returns. How much is it also a requirement of an individual CA to 'police' the activities and possible HMRC submissions of others in relation to cash transactions?*

Is there any further information (including legal obligations) or discussion that might be relevant?

Depending on the responses to raising concerns with the Managing Director some form of 'whistleblowing' may be necessary. You may need to seek legal advice as to duties and obligations in the context of business and professional relationships under the Public Interest Disclosure legislation.

Is there a conflict between the 'Guardian' and 'Commercial' strands of an accountant's responsibilities?

In this situation, the 'Commercial' practices of the business need to be constrained by 'Guardian' expectations.

Based on the information available, is there scope for an imaginative solution?

Not obviously - although there seem compelling grounds that the business should review both its accounting and sales practices for reputational risk with regards to the completeness and accuracy of its own submissions to HMRC and in its dealings with the general public.

Using the cash float for personal convenience, while not illegal, would seem an inappropriate act.

Are there any other comments?

The previous Financial Controller appears to have become overly 'familiar' with the role and accepted the false accounting by the Managing Director over cash.

This recently qualified Financial Controller/Company secretary has a challenging and lonely position and would seem well advised to get early advice from his/her professional body.

Whilst changing retail practices, such as use of the internet, may negate the effectiveness and techniques such as 'the violin', the underlying ethical issues could be replicated in other ways.

Scenario 8: The directors' unofficial loan account

How great this job had first seemed! Having recently moved to a relatively remote coastal town in order to fit in with your spouse's career, you had waited for many months to find an appropriate, accounting-related post. You were, therefore, both very pleased, and relieved, to have been appointed, albeit on a probationary basis, as 'Finance Director' at a well-known, local private company. This has, as its principal asset, a victorian hotel, together with various tourism-linked operations.

The owner-directors, a husband and wife, who are actively engaged in the day-to-day running of the business, have been very co-operative over organising flexible working hours to suit you. You get on well with the staff and the job has helped you settle surprisingly readily into the local community, where the proprietors are clearly popular and well respected.

They had inherited the hotel some years ago, then in a run-down state, and invested much money, time and effort in trying not just to restore it but also to develop supplementary activities. Realistically, with the long term decline of tourism in this region, the business as a commercial operation will probably only ever be marginal. You understand that the company had faced some serious cash flow difficulties in the recent past. However, a re-mortgaging arrangement just before you came has, apparently, eased up on the financial pressures. It is now mid-April. Easter trading was better than expected. There is a reasonable stream of advanced bookings for the summer and some useful deposits for weddings through to the autumn. The company is currently well below its overdraft limits and should remain so for many months ahead.

The Managing Director comes to you with a company cheque for £4,000 that he has already signed. He asks for your counter-signature. Grinning slightly, he explains that it is the deposit necessary to cover design work and furnishings for new hotel bedrooms. There is a formal invoice for this from a design studio, Auxen Designs (2001) Ltd.

('Auxen'). This request and payment surprises you greatly. You were not aware that any such outlays had been discussed, planned or budgeted for by the board. Admittedly, you have yet to attend a board meeting, but since the only other directors are the Managing Director and his wife, Dorothy, it seems very odd that they should not have mentioned such a significant matter, if only informally. Despite your puzzlement, nevertheless, given the Managing Director's prior authorisation, the invoice and the relatively small sum, you smile and sign.

However, you decide that you should investigate it a little further. While available details are sparse, you find that Auxen has a year-end of 30 April and appears in the past to have a high level of indebtedness. You note the name of Dorothy's adult daughter as the company secretary.

You are still trying to work out how to raise the matter with the Managing Director when, two days later, he comes with another cheque, this time for £25,000, again needing only your counter-signature. Again there is a supporting invoice from Auxen Ltd. You are clearly hesitant and the Managing Director comments that he is only asking you to sign because Dorothy is away today and it is important to get the cheque away promptly so that it can be banked ahead of 30 April.

You ask why there is the rush, given that there is no evidence of any design work having started. You also point out that you have consistently tried to keep bank balances as favourable as possible.

The Managing Director laughs and replies that the money should be back in the hotel bank account by later in the summer. He explains that the cheques are needed urgently to settle outstanding directors' loan accounts at the design studio company, especially over its year-end. Once this has passed, the money should find its way back to the hotel company, though it may need a bit of negotiation with Auxen's creditors. He adds:

> *Meanwhile, Auxen's accountant suggested we take out loans here and put the other side of the accounting entry into a fixed asset,*

'bedroom development', account. Putting it 'to bed' as it were, for a couple of months or so, should give us the fewest possible tax and accounting problems. Directors' loans are not illegal - just messy for tax.

Apparently, by doing it this way, the entries can readily be reversed out when 'our' loan is repaid in due course. If challenged, we can always say that the directors have just changed their minds over the developments.

He adds that Dorothy will be back tomorrow and can sign the cheque if you really feel that you must refuse. However, he makes it clear that he finds your reluctance to sign surprising, unhelpful and disappointing.

You are conscious that he and Dorothy have been generally very kind and helpful to you. You are mindful that you are still on probation; there were several other well-qualified applicants for the post and good opportunities are rare. Within the local community there will be surprise and little sympathy if you have managed to fall out with the popular owners of a significant local employer.

What do you do now?

Scenario 8: Analysis

What are the readily-identifiable ethical issues for your decision?

For you personally

Do you accept invoices for non-existent capital expenditure in order to mask a loan being made to directors?

How do you counter the loneliness and isolation of decision-making - whether dealing with friendly or bullying superiors - where there are few alternatives available and where 'false accounting' seems to be part of the chosen solution?

By addressing the underlying problem and using your technical skills, can you find an acceptable alternative?

Who are the key parties who can influence, or will be affected by, your decision?

'You' (and your family); the Managing Director and Dorothy; Auxen's accountant; HMRC.

What fundamental ethical principles for accountants are most applicable and is there an apparent conflict between them?

Integrity	*How to insist on a level of truthfulness within the accounting function when there are significant personal pressures and incentives to accept an arrangement that involves invidious (rather than blatant) dishonesty that has been presented as a norm or 'given'.*
Objectivity	*How to concentrate - without being distracted - on finding a persuasive solution to the underlying problem.*
Professional competence and due care	*Firstly, seeking to use professional and technical skills to find a legal means of lending money from one company to another that does not involve deception. Secondly, communicating criticism of the 'false accounting' - apparently proposed by another accountant - in a way that is effective in securing an alternative solution.*
Confidentiality	*Assumed.*
Professional behaviour	*How, courteously but firmly, to uphold accepted standards of financial reporting and compliance with tax regulations.*

Is there any further information (including legal obligations) or discussion that might be relevant?

What is the nature of the problem at Auxen and what are the implications, formal and informal, for the business where you are Financial Director?

Loans between companies are not illegal (provided it is not against the interests of creditors) although loans to directors that would otherwise be payments as dividends or salaries have tax consequences. Making a loan to Auxen should be possible - assuming that it is acceptable to the bank - without subterfuge being adopted. There will be tax consequences but these need not necessarily be adverse.

Is there a conflict between the 'Guardian' and 'Commercial' strands of an accountant's responsibilities?

Although it may seem daunting, in both your 'Commercial' and 'Guardian' roles you need to encourage the directors to explore legal ways to assist Auxen that do not jeopardise their own business.

Based on the information available, is there scope for an imaginative solution?

There should be.

Are there any other comments?

You need to use interpersonal skills in a non-confrontational way to offer to find a solution to the underlying problem.

There must be concerns that the Managing Director and Dorothy were apparently prepared to countenance false accounting but this gives an incentive to address the underlying problem in a constructive way.

Scenario 9: Unhealthy foods

Over a number of years you have acted as auditor and financial adviser to a family company. It was formed out of a partnership, founded by the husband and wife team of Walter and Marjorie. The business operates in the 'health food' sector with three main activities:

- retailing, with five shops, three in Glasgow and two in Edinburgh;
- wholesaling and distributing to smaller independents, primarily in the Glasgow area; and
- muesli-mixing, with a low scale milling unit based in East Lothian. It produces a range of breakfast cereals (from plain through to exotic) largely to match specific orders from the company's own or other independent shops.

The business has only ever been moderately profitable but it has enabled the two owner-directors to live a comfortable, if modest, lifestyle.

After a lacklustre university career and what his parents euphemistically call a 'gap year' - it was nearer five! - Walter and Marjorie persuaded their only child, Nathan, to come into the business. Progressively, they have given him more responsibility. As of five years ago, he manages the 'Eastern' activities (the two Edinburgh shops and the mill) while his parents manage the 'Western' activities. Although not a director, Nathan receives a substantially larger salary than either of his parents. He, his wife and two small children live in a large and comfortable steading, situated close by the mill but also in ready commuting distance to the shops and facilities of Edinburgh.

There have been some attempts to enhance internal controls by setting up separate cost/profit centres but these arrangements remain rudimentary. Too often, the movement of goods between the seven locations goes unregistered for the records to be consistently reliable so that the company operates more a 'common pot' approach to management accounting.

This year's draft financial statements have shown a sharp fall into a loss that neither Walter, Marjorie or Nathan seem able to explain. Sales and market conditions have, if anything, been more buoyant than in the past and costs levels have merely kept pace with inflation. Audit performance indicators highlight a deterioration in gross margin but because of the 'common pot' it is difficult to be more specific as to why.

Nevertheless, the audit team member reviewing turnover had noted a substantial rise in sales from the mill and the Edinburgh shops to one customer, Bristol Beaufoods Ltd. Following up on the performance indicators, she had undertaken various price comparisons and determined that the majority of transactions with this customer appeared to be at, or below, cost. Moreover, on closer examination of goods delivered/sales invoices, together with calculations based on the mill's production records, it appears Bristol Beaufoods Ltd has been sold more of the lowest cost type of muesli than has been produced. By contrast, other investigations of purchases show that the mill has bought in much more than previously of higher-priced ingredients. The team's conclusion is that Bristol Beaufoods Ltd is not only receiving substantial discounts from the Edinburgh shops but being sold the mill's premium products for the price of the lowest in the range.

These provisional findings were discussed with Nathan who had become notably more elusive as the audit progressed. Independently, you arranged that a member of the audit team quantify the impact of these transactions. It is readily demonstrable that without these trades, a profitable outcome (rather than the provisional loss) would have been achieved. This revised profit would have been significantly higher than in the previous year, but then this too may have been depressed by similar deals. Separately you arranged for a company search on Bristol

Beaufoods Ltd. This revealed that its two shareholders are Nathan and his wife. It has been trading for three years and appears to be reasonably profitable - perhaps not surprisingly given its advantageous purchasing arrangements.

Hence, you now have evidence to substantiate allegations against Nathan, and possibly his wife also, of stealing from his parents. However, you are under no delusions as to just how painful the revelation of this situation will be for Walter and Marjorie - fond parents (if perhaps overly so) and adoring grandparents. Nor will explaining these accusations be pleasant for Nathan and his wife. Short and long-term, family relationships may be irrevocably damaged.

Although fraud investigation was not a specific remit, the information is material for the audit and potentially relevant for tax computations. You decide that, having identified malpractice by a senior staff member, there is no alternative but that the directors/shareholders are made aware of the circumstances promptly.

However, do you raise these first with Walter and Marjorie, or do you give Nathan some prior warning? In that way, he can prepare for the exposure, perhaps, allowing him to tell his parents himself and having ready some proposal for restitution that might mitigate the damage to family relationships.

What do you do now?

Scenario 9: Analysis

What are the readily-identifiable ethical issues for your decision?

For you personally

Does the nature of your client's circumstances and relationships cause you to modify usual expectations for confidentiality?

For the CA firm

Is there a supportive environment for discussion of practical dilemmas?

Who are the key parties who can influence, or will be affected by, your decision?

Only 'you' for the decision. Walter and Marjorie; Nathan and his family will all be directly affected. Other staff may be indirectly affected.

What fundamental ethical principles for accountants are most applicable and is there an apparent conflict between them?

Integrity	*Your interests and that of your client(s) coincide in terms of making your relationship as sensitive and friendly as possible in difficult circumstances - but how much discretion do you have in deciding what your clients' best interests are?*
Objectivity	*How confident are you that any decision you make will exclude any personal feelings of: • repugnance over Nathan's actions; • wishing to claim full credit for discovery with your client, but concentrate on what are the best interests of the parties, directly and indirectly, involved?*
Professional competence and due care	*Assumed.*
Confidentiality	*At present you have complete control of the information because of the competence and diligence of your staff's audit work. Expectations of confidentiality are that you would report firstly to the directors but should you risk not following this to reflect the circumstances?*
Professional behaviour	*How can your respect for the interests of others be most effectively demonstrated in practice? Do you at this stage need to consider the impact on other staff at the Scottish business or at Bristol Beaufoods Ltd?*

Is there any further information (including legal obligations) or discussion that might be relevant?

No. Encouraging Nathan to 'confess' promptly to his parents - with the clear understanding that if he does not, you will be disclosing anyway - does not seem to constitute 'tipping off' in the legal meaning of the definition. The potentially complex implications for taxation of what has occurred will still need consideration and reporting, but are unaffected by the immediate issue of timing.

Is there a conflict between the 'Guardian' and 'Commercial' strands of an accountant's responsibilities?

While sensitivity with others may seem more of a 'Commercial' attribute than the more harshly disciplining approach expected of a 'Guardian' perspective, consideration for others can be a shared value. Longer-term, there are issues to be explored over the need to respect boundaries on 'Confidentiality' for the preservation both of good order ('Guardian') and of trust ('Commerce').

Based on the information available, is there scope for an imaginative solution?

No, beyond giving Nathan an opportunity to prepare his parents for the revelation and, perhaps, allowing them to perceive that he has 'confessed'.

Are there any other comments?

As often, the contentious ethical issues are affected by the nature of relationships. In the original, source circumstances, the parents were presented with the information and evidence shortly ahead of a pre-arranged meeting with their son, who had not been warned.

Scenario 10: Foreign corrupt practices

You are based as an expatriate, salaried partner at the Middle Eastern office of a major international firm where you lead the engagement of the subsidiary of a US multinational. The board of the parent company has set demanding ethical policies and standards, also making these prominent in its profile for international advertising. Each member of its staff has had to return documentation under the multinational's own 'Ethical Conduct Program' and the US Foreign Corrupt Practices Act ['FCPA'] to confirm that they have engaged in no illegal or unethical conduct in the course of their employment. There were no negative returns and now, you, yourself, on behalf of your firm, have in front of you various certificates to sign confirming that you are aware of no instances of failure to conform to these policies.

However, consistent with your firm's practice licence within the host country, you are also engagement partner for a local supplier to the US subsidiary. This is a relatively small but regionally-based company that is respected both as efficient and as 'well-connected' to influential local families. It has been a client for some years, although, according to rumour, its proprietors have few inhibitions about continuing what they see as long-standing and culturally acceptable practices for generous gift-giving as part of normal business negotiations. You, yourself have a good working relationship with the senior managers who combine charm with a shrewd commercial acumen. At no stage has there been any hint of asking you to exchange any favours.

Last week, during the on-going audit of the local company, one of your staff involved with the audits of both clients discovered among the board papers a list of 'arrangements' that, in US terms, could only be described as 'bribes'. Although personal names could not be identified (only synonyms and numbered bank accounts at 'off-shore' centres were given for individual recipients) those of their employing companies were clearly stated. That of your US subsidiary client features prominently.

A check has shown that the amounts and dates of payments match the company's banking records. The unavoidable fact is you have been shown highly credible grounds for believing that deliberate breaches of the 'Ethical Conduct Program' and the FCPA have occurred, and are continuing, at the US subsidiary, quite possibly amongst its most senior executives.

You expect that the local proprietors will confirm, when asked for audit representation purposes, the acceptability to themselves of the payments and amounts made by their senior managers. These are not illegal and have no significant tax implications. However, you have every expectation that, were you to ask, the proprietors would flatly refuse to furnish you with any further details of the payees. Moreover, they could well take offence that you had asked them to do so. Although the giving of financial inducements to the US subsidiary's staff is in direct breach of contracts, there is no local precedent or mechanism for enforcement, let alone of penalties.

Were you to threaten to resign from this audit to try to force the proprietors or senior managers to disclose to you precise names, you believe it could seriously damage, not enhance, your firm's practice within the host country and regional business community. You have heard, anecdotally, of a partner in a competitor firm who had confidentially notified a US Head Office of ethical breaches only to have the subsequent visiting US investigators carelessly reveal their source. Thereafter, apparently branded as a 'troublemaker' he had left the region before completing his contract. As a salaried partner, you know that you too are, in effect, 'on probation' for a possible equity partnership in the UK and 'troublemaker' seems an epithet best avoided!

Your staff member was clearly very proud of uncovering the list and making the connection. He asked you earlier today what you are going to do about it and the signing of the certificates.

What do you do now?

Scenario 10: Analysis

What are the readily-identifiable ethical issues for your decision?

For you personally

Can/should information coincidently obtained by you in your capacity as auditor at one company influence the professional opinion that you are required to give at another?

Is there an irreconcilable conflict between 'integrity' and an approach to 'objectivity' that sees clients as operating in 'silos'?

How do you balance professional commitments between two very different cultural frameworks, where there are different ethical expectations and traditions?

How do you explain your decision to your staff member? Or, perhaps in due course, to your family?

For the CA firm

How do you support partners and staff to explore openly the different ethical dilemmas, expectations and traditions within international networks?

Who are the key parties who can influence, or will be affected by, your decision?

'You', your fellow partners, including the engagement partner for the US Holding company. However, they are, in effect, an extension of yourself and cannot change the underlying fundamentals of the problem. The local

proprietors and their managers could assist you, although you believe that they will be unwilling to help and offended if asked to do so.

Your staff member is directly affected now, as, potentially, your family will be. Affected, wittingly or not, are the FCPA Regulators, together with shareholders and directors of the parent company and senior management of the subsidiary.

What fundamental ethical principles for accountants are most applicable and is there an apparent conflict between them?

Integrity	*Self-interest (as a junior, salaried partner) may give a strong incentive to ignore what is a coincidental discovery but can/should you sign a certificate specifically confirming compliance when there are very strong grounds, but not the legal proof of details of names, to suggest breaches by a client's employees of their legal obligations and conditions of employment?*
Objectivity	*To what extent are you balancing an inclination to impress (by showing your audit investigative abilities) with a reticence to avoid embarrassing your firm through appearing as overly zealous in policing laws/ethical standards that have limited local acceptance?*
Professional competence and due care	*Assumed.*
Confidentiality	*Can/should you use privileged information at one client to inform your duties at another?*
Professional behaviour	*To what extent can you reconcile duties of confidentiality in respect of individual clients, with expectations of wider public service, including the upholding of compliance with contracts?*

Is there any further information (including legal obligations) or discussion that might be relevant?

Not for the purposes of discussing the principles of this problem.

Is there a conflict between the 'Guardian' and 'Commercial' strands of an accountant's responsibilities?

Yes, in that from a 'commercial' perspective you are likely to give more sympathy to local business conventions that allow for the exchange of favours between agents within business negotiations. In a 'Guardian' capacity, it is disturbing to contemplate knowingly having to give an inaccurate certification and knowing yourself to have been 'deceived' as an upholder of legality and contracts. Moreover, your employment and presence as an expatriate is to show experience and loyalty to the standards that the US holding company is seeking to impose. Your staff member expects leadership in the 'Guardian' role from you.

Based on the information available, is there scope for an imaginative solution?

While respecting the confidentiality and identity of your local client, advise your US contacts informally that there are grounds of suspicion of bribe receipts by some staff. Although this is an incomplete solution, it establishes as a 'known' (with some quantification even though the full evidence is not available) the fact of the continuity of the problem of bribe-taking, despite the existence of policies. However, this has the risk for you of triggering some potentially heavy-handed investigation.

Are there any other comments?

Would the situation be different, if the list had given dates and amounts remitted to offshore bank accounts that matched actual names of individuals at the US subsidiary? Would the situation be different if you had discovered the connection yourself without this also being in the knowledge of any of your staff?

There are some parallels in this scenario with the issues in scenarios 16 and 21.

Scenario 11: Interim results

You are the lead audit partner for a FTSE 100 group that has an extensive range of overseas activities. You have established a good working relationship with each of the Finance Director (FD), the Group Chairman and the senior non-executive who chairs the Group Audit Committee. However, it is some years since the audit was last put out to tender and you are aware that this is likely within the next eighteen months.

Three years ago, the group embarked upon a significant acquisition in Canada. The FD had been a keen advocate of this initiative and was appointed to chair the new subsidiary by the Group's main board. Although the initial purchase price was comparatively low, the subsequent cashflows for research and development in a fast changing industry have been considerable and significantly higher than first budgeted.

Ahead of your firm's independent review of the Group's six-monthly, interim report, the FD asked to speak to you in strict confidence. He explained that, as chair of the Canadian subsidiary, he believes that further difficulties will emerge that will be more intractable and expensive than have already been reported to the main board and to the stock markets. However, it is still very difficult to quantify what the further costs will be. He accepted that the value of the investment has been impaired, to the extent that some write-off, material to the group, will be necessary. However, the situation is still very fluid.

The FD cited to you the relevant guidance in the Accounting Standards that no impairment should be booked until it is known with reasonable certainty. While an eventual write-down, probably at the coming year-end, is near certain, he has not yet quantified the amount. In his opinion, no disclosure should be made at this, the interim, stage because amounts are too uncertain.

You acknowledged what he had told you but asked to reserve judgement. You ponder that the 'Review Conclusion' which you will need to sign, will state:

> *On the basis of our review we are not aware of any material modifications that should be made to the financial information as presented for the six months ended…*

Within hours, the Group Chairman phoned to organise an urgent meeting, also on a strictly confidential basis. Immediately you met, it is clear that he has been told, but only in very general terms, by the FD of the impairment issue together with the FD's intention to defer disclosure. He and the FD have had a strained relationship and now he is shocked and angry. He wants counter arguments from you as to why the impairment must be included in the six monthly reporting. Referring to the FD, he says:

> *I am going to tell him publicly that there are no other instances where the FD of a FTSE 100 company disagrees with its auditors. You must assert that the auditors require a rapid quantification of the impairment, forthwith!*

What do you do now?

Scenario 11: Analysis

What are the readily-identifiable ethical issues for your decision?

For you personally

How can you ensure that you (and the directors) fully comply with an auditor's (and directors') duties to shareholders in relation to current knowledge of price sensitive information, in a manner that retains the respect of both (rival) directors?

The ethical issues have arisen because there were imposed circumstances of strict confidentiality between individual 'stakeholders', whereas there ought to be informed debate among the board members over whether or not to disclose. The imposition was reasonable when requested. However, should you now release yourself from the constraints? Is there a separate ethical obligation to persuade both parties to communicate more effectively and co-operatively to concentrate on the wider and different stakeholder interests, not just within management but those of shareholders and prospective shareholders?

How do you maintain objectivity if either the FD or the Group Chairman were to imply a threat to you/your firm within the expected tender process?

For the CA firm

Is there a supportive environment for discussion of practical dilemmas involving relationships where professional integrity may be questioned?

Who are the key parties who can influence, or will be affected by, your decision?

'You'; the FD; Group Chairman; users and potential users of the financial statements.

What fundamental ethical principles for accountants are most applicable and is there an apparent conflict between them?

Integrity	*How do you decide on the most appropriate way of moving the debate towards a constructive conclusion while retaining respect for your objectivity by both parties?*
Objectivity	*How do you maintain a concentration on the facts and technical issues relating to the practicability, or otherwise, of disclosure, rather than issues of personality and the prospective audit tender?*
Professional competence and due care	*Assumed. Detailed knowledge of technical requirements must be a fundamental pre-requisite to having the responsibility for giving of advice.*
Confidentiality	*How do you ensure that both parties continue to trust you as someone with whom they can discuss their concerns?*
Professional behaviour	*You have a professional and public-service duty that, when signing the certificate, you believe the directors' decisions have been made through a process that combines integrity, objectivity, competence and diligence - even if the FD and Group Chairman may show each other little courtesy.*

Is there any further information (including legal obligations) or discussion that might be relevant?

While in practice you would need to be fully familiar with the detailed wording on impairment and identification, this does not impinge on the over-riding ethical issues.

Is there a conflict between the 'Guardian' and 'Commercial' strands of an accountant's responsibilities?

You are operating in a 'Guardian' capacity seeking to facilitate the resolution of the argument in a manner that gives the most appropriate disclosure to the stakeholders, in terms of the investment community and wider public. The 'commercial' pressures on you over re-appointment must be secondary to fulfilling the 'Guardian' role. If you perform the 'Guardian' role well, this should give you the 'Commercial' reward, although this cannot be guaranteed.

Based on the information available, is there scope for an imaginative solution?

Tell both parties that this needs to be discussed openly at the Audit Committee and seek their permission for you to contact the chair of the Audit Committee to arrange this.

Are there any other comments?

The ethical issues are integral to those of developing and sustaining relationships. There are some similarities in this scenario with the situation in scenario 17 'How much do you tell the FD?'. In scenario 11, as the statutorily-appointed auditor required to provide an objective opinion, you can more readily act as a facilitator and enabler. You can use the established respect for the auditor position (especially here where you have two good working relationships) to go to the Audit Committee and help broker an outcome that acknowledges the competing concerns. The Professional behaviour obligation is that you deliver this useful public service whatever your expectations from the internal politics of the board.

Scenario 12: Poor charity!

You are the audit partner of a charitable group that is structured to include a wholly-owned trading company. The company's profits are covenanted to be paid over annually to the charity, which provides widely-valued public services. Your firm also acts as the group's tax adviser.

The audit team has discovered, just a week too late, that, for a prior period, no cheque was raised for the transfer of the covenanted funds, nor was the appropriate documentation prepared within the regulatory deadlines. Tax will therefore be payable and it is likely to be irrecoverable.

There is some uncertainty as to whether the charity's staff, or your own taxation advisory staff, were responsible for the oversight. It is not stipulated in the letter of engagement but in every previous year since the covenant was set up, your firm has written to the charity reminding its accountant of the deadline. On this occasion, no such prompting was given, probably due to a change of staff at your firm.

You describe this situation to the charity's Chief Executive Officer who is clearly very concerned about what has happened. She talks gloomily of having to cut services and lay off staff - unless HMRC allow a late claim, or the charity can successfully sue your firm. Suddenly, she brightens up and suggests the simple solution. The documentation should be back-dated and submitted now, and the tax return should be prepared consistent with this earlier dating. As she says:

> *After all everything we are doing is fully in keeping with the spirit of what society wants; what the politicians encourage and the tax rules allow - surely 'common sense' must prevail!*

What do you do now?

Scenario 12: Analysis

What are the readily-identifiable ethical issues for your decision?

For you personally

Can you exercise any 'ethical' discretion in this? Or, must you explain that motives and intentions in taxation matters cannot prevail over facts. Hence, the timing of when the cheque was, or was not, cleared is the critical criterion so that you and your firm cannot be party to the submission of documentation that has been back-dated in the manner suggested.

Who is responsible? - is this a factor that could affect your objectivity?

For the CA firm

Is there a supportive environment for open discussion of practical dilemmas without a recriminatory, or 'blame', culture?

Who are the key parties who can influence, or will be affected by, your decision?

'You'; a decision-maker at HMRC; the charity and its beneficiaries and (potentially) your firm.

What fundamental ethical principles for accountants are most applicable and is there an apparent conflict between them?

Integrity	*Can you accept the 'common sense' argument for back-dating of documents?*
Objectivity	*How do you ignore the possibility that your firm may be responsible so that even if it cannot be successfully sued, significant amounts of time, energy and goodwill could be expended in defending this?*
Professional competence and due care	*Whether or not exercised in the recent past, not now a key issue.*
Confidentiality	*Not a key issue.*
Professional behaviour	*How do you keep in mind the long term damage that an accepted practice of 'back-dating' may cause?*

Is there any further information (including legal obligations) or discussion that might be relevant?

Arrangements over covenanting may have changed but the principles have not.

Is there a conflict between the 'Guardian' and 'Commercial' strands of an accountant's responsibilities?

The 'Commercial' argument would be to accept the intended substance of the arrangement over the detailed legal form of the dating. However, in a 'Guardian' capacity, back-dating a legal document to reverse an error (whoever made it) seems a dangerous precedent and appears to risk ill-discipline.

Based on the information available, is there scope for an imaginative solution?

Attempting the same outcome by legitimate means, such as explaining to HMRC and seeing if there can be any discretion whereby the covenanted funds can still be transferred. However, no such flexibility may be possible.

Are there any other comments?

No

Scenario 13: Obligations to disclose

The problem is that I have just kept putting it off! What I want now is to start with a clean slate. I first started buying and selling gold coins held offshore six years ago. I didn't disclose the details to your firm or to HMRC because I thought that as currency they were exempt from tax. Then three years ago, I learned that this had to be disclosed as trading. But at the time my wife had just been diagnosed with cancer. Things drifted and another couple of years slipped by before I started to think about it seriously. My quick calculations show the numbers to be alarmingly large. I am not sure now that I have readily available the cash resources to pay the back tax, penalties and fines etc. Quite frankly too, with the business really taking off, I don't have time for all the hassle. I only do very few trades of the coins now. I am willing to start off as new but I don't want any delving into the past.

It was nine months ago that, as an experienced audit senior manager, you heard this at the end of a one-to-one audit meeting with Ricky, the Managing Director of a well-established family business. Other siblings are directors and shareholders. There is a company accountant who is not a family member.

Not being a tax specialist you offered no immediate advice but, as your firm deals with Ricky's personal tax return, you passed on details of the conversation to the engagement partner, Simon. His response had included a more than usual number of expletives. Shortly afterwards, Simon told you that he had made clear to Ricky in a private meeting that, unless he agreed fully to disclose to HMRC the transactions with offshore coins, the firm would have to sever all professional ties in relation to Ricky's financial affairs. Both you and Simon are disappointed, and not just from the loss of fees. Ricky is a pleasant and interesting client, skilfully taking the leading role in developing a successful, growing business. In all other business matters he has always been reliable. The origins of this tax problem seem to have been a genuine mistake.

Apparently, Ricky had asked Simon for more time to think about the situation. You surmise that there was also another, very short, meeting between the two. However, you do now know that Ricky has approached another firm of CAs that has taken on his, and his immediate family's, personal tax and finance work. However, your firm has retained the corporate responsibilities, although the company accountant hinted that the directors are considering moving these to the other firm.

After some hesitation, you have asked Simon how the professional obligations to report known omissions to HMRC and under the Proceeds of Crime Act had been discharged. Simon responds that he considers it sufficient that another CA firm now deals with Ricky's personal tax matters. He goes on:

I am satisfied that we have acted very professionally. We have lost a valuable personal tax client in upholding a matter of principle and we have probably put 'at risk' a long-standing audit relationship with an even more valuable corporate client. Personally, I don't think there is any need to go further. The corporate client is not just Ricky - there are other directors and shareholders. What sort of explanation could we give to them if we decided to resign? And we don't need to force them to sack us by souring relations with the Managing Director. I agreed with Ricky not to contact HMRC and that no reference to the past trading in offshore coins would be made in the professional clearances to the other firm.

This seems only fair. Ricky told me that had he had any inkling that his telling you about the offshore coins was not covered by strict professional confidentiality, he would never have raised the subject with you except, perhaps, in hypothetical terms. He feels that he has the basic human right at least to have been warned against 'incriminating himself.

Given this misunderstanding and that we have no specific details in written form, I think that neither I, nor you, nor the firm have any further ethical obligations. Dealing with the offshore coins is now an issue for Ricky and his new advisers. With the company, there are checks and balances provided by other directors. Basically, I trust Ricky as an honest person who unintentionally made a one-off error and then let this one matter slip when he had many bigger preoccupations.

Ricky knows that I am very keen to keep the audit. Since you raise the subject, I must say, I think it is very important that Ricky should not feel awkward in his contacts with you. Do you think it would be better all round if you transferred your responsibilities on the audit to another senior manager?

What do you do now?

Scenario 13: Analysis

What are the readily identifiable ethical issues for your decision?

For you personally

In this scenario you believe that the firm which employs you, despite its resignation, has not complied fully with HMRC guidance. In that you are aware of this, albeit tax is not your speciality, do you see yourself as ethically compromised in relation to the firm's professional duties to inform? Should you act independently, or be seeking advice from your firm's ethics partner, under the security of confidentiality, as to what you should do personally to remedy the omissions? Or do you quietly ignore the situation?

Do you consider Simon's suggestion, that you transfer audit responsibilities, to be appropriate?

For the CA firm

From an ethics perspective, is it acting with integrity to have accepted Ricky's arguments on the basis that had he known of the professional disclosure requirements, he would not have given anyone in the firm details relating to the overseas coins?

Is the distinction between what is spoken and what is written relevant from an ethical perspective?

Is the legal distinction between resigning from dealing with Ricky's (and his family's) personal tax affairs and continuing to act for the company acceptable from an ethical standpoint?

With regards to the legal perspective, see under 'further information'.

Who are the key parties who can influence, or will be affected by, your decision?

'You'; Simon; your firm; the new tax advisers; HMRC; Ricky; Ricky's fellow directors and the other shareholders.

What fundamental ethical principles for accountants are most applicable and is there an apparent conflict between them?

Integrity	*Do you consider that your own integrity has been compromised by how the firm/Simon have responded to Ricky's informal disclosure?* *Does the fact that the information was received only orally have any significance?*
Objectivity	*Do you consider that the firm's objectivity is irrevocably compromised because of what Simon and you know regarding Ricky's tax situation?* *How do you assess whether to take up Simon's suggestion of a transfer of client responsibilities?*
Professional competence and due care	*Assumed.*
Confidentiality	*How valid is the argument that Ricky should have been warned by you about the limits to professional confidentiality immediately he started telling you about the overseas coins?*
Professional behaviour	*Is there an over-riding public duty on you as an individual that has not been fully satisfied?*

Is there any further information (including legal obligations) or discussion that might be relevant?

Additional to exploration as to ethical responses, consideration is necessary as to legal disclosure requirements under HMRC Guidance and/or current legislation (e.g. the Proceeds of Crime Act 2002 or Serious Organised Crime and Police Act 2005) where tax returns that have been submitted by a firm on behalf of a client are now known to be incomplete.

Is there a conflict between the 'Guardian' and 'Commercial' strands of an accountant's responsibilities?

Yes. The' Guardian' role would police the law; the 'Commercial' inclination is to maintain good working relationships - for you personally with your employing firm and for the firm with a valued corporate client, where there is a basic trust of the individual involved.

Based on the information available, is there scope for an imaginative solution?

Discussion with the firm's ethics partner may give you guidance. The offer to transfer you from the audit does not address the underlying ethical issues.

Are there any other comments?

The original of this scenario pre-dated the Proceeds of Crime Act 2002, and subsequent guidance, so that the situation is now more legally proscribed but the underlying ethical issues remain worth discussing.

Scenario 14: Can the 'withholding tax' be recovered?

You are a taxation partner in a multi-practice international firm that acts as auditor and tax adviser to a successful, privately-owned company, OmniedRD plc ['OmniedRD']. This recruits, employs and manages teams of specialist and technical staff for overseas assignments under contracts with clients in the extractive industries. Its growth record and public profile makes it a particularly valued client at your office.

Reviewing submission of its UK tax computation prior to submission, you see a reference to a 10% withholding tax paid in respect of transactions with its South American subsidiary. You ask your staff for further details and, after some enquiries, OmniedRD's own accountant phones you to explain.

Some years ago, OmniedRD had sought to expand its operations in South America. It remitted capital funds for its existing, wholly-owned subsidiary to open a branch office in a provincial city. At a critical and very late stage, local politicians there had demanded bribes, in the form of requests for unnecessary work permits at inflated rates. With regret, but as a matter of ethical principle, the UK directors decided this was not acceptable and cancelled the branch project. The bulk of the funds for the aborted expansion were not spent. The existing subsidiary has continued to trade successfully.

Since then the capital remittance of US $1,500,000 has remained in the subsidiary's South American bank account. Permission to repatriate monies relating to capital sums/loans is very slow, due to restrictive legislation and bureaucracy. Indeed, despite costly legal representations there is still no date set for their release, or even information as to when that might be. By contrast, permission for remittances in respect of operational activities is much easier to obtain, albeit subject to a 10% withholding tax.

Last year, having made an unexpected group loss and needing the US $1,500,000 with some urgency for investment elsewhere, OmniedRD's UK owners/directors lost patience with the delays and expense of the repatriation process. With the informal agreement of their subsidiary's management, five separate 'dummy' invoices were raised by the UK holding company for 'technical services'. These have matched the US $1,500,000. Payment for these has been settled, subject to US $150,000 being withheld. While resenting the need for the deduction, the UK owner/directors consider that this is an acceptable method for early access to the funds, even though it is their own money that they have sought to release.

The five 'dummy' invoices have been excluded from turnover and the remittances have been treated as re-payment of the existing inter-company loan.

The client's accountant thinks that there is a legitimate claim for double tax relief in the UK, in that the withholding tax had actually been paid. He can show you the bona fide receipts for this. When you point out that because these are based on false invoices it could constitute a fraud on HMRC, the client's accountant suggests that the US $150,000 should still be claimed, as an expense if not as a tax. It is, in effect, the write-off of a part of an inter-company loan.

While not material in terms of group turnover, the owner/directors consider US$150,000 to be significant and that, ethically, they are entitled to relief from UK taxes for the sum that they have paid irrecoverably to the South American government.

He asks you to write to him if you are going to recommend any other treatment than claiming the withheld tax in full.

What do you do now?

Scenario 14: Analysis

What are the readily-identifiable ethical issues for your decision?

For you personally

Should you:

1) *accept the 'dummy invoices' as a misrepresentation but one validated by the circumstances;*
2) *argue for a less specific 'write off' of expenses (unsupported by the receipts);*
3) *press that no claim for recovering the US$150,000 be made in the UK so that there is no need to refer to any aspect of the transaction in returns or correspondence with HMRC?*

If you decide on 3), do you raise this matter with your audit colleagues and urge them to contact the auditors of the subsidiary in South America?

If you decide on 3), should you report the creation of 'dummy invoices' by the client's accountant to his/her professional institute?

For the CA firm

How do you support partners and staff to explore openly the different ethical dilemmas, expectations and traditions within international networks?

Who are the key parties who can influence, or will be affected, by your decision?

'You'; the client's accountant ; the other owner/directors; HMRC; the local managers of the South American subsidiary; the auditors in the UK and of the subsidiary; and the South American authorities.

What fundamental ethical principles for accountants are most applicable and is there an apparent conflict between them?

Integrity	*Can you accept, in the circumstances described, your forwarding to HMRC what you know to be 'dummy invoices'?*
Objectivity	*How do you remain uninfluenced by the importance of this client to your office/firm?*
Professional competence and due care	*Assumed, and that you are seeking to maintain professional standards.*
Confidentiality	*What are your responsibilities in making your discovery known to audit colleagues, in the UK and in South America?*
Professional behaviour	*What are your obligations in relation to HMRC and the South American authorities?*

Is there any further information (including legal obligations) or discussion that might be relevant?

The details of the laws in this situation do not alter the underlying ethical dilemma.

Is there a conflict between the 'Guardian' and 'Commercial' strands of an accountant's responsibilities?

The 'Commercial' pressure is not to challenge an arrangement that would accept the substance over form. The 'Guardian' responsibility recoils at the preparation of financial documents knowingly prepared in order to deceive other 'Guardians'.

Based on the information available, is there scope for an imaginative solution?

Not obvious.

Are there any other comments?

Does it make a difference to you as to whether the South American auditors are part of your own firm's international network, or not?

Scenario 15: Should the social security be paid?

You are the same taxation partner as in scenario 14 with the international multi-practice firm that acts as auditor and tax adviser to the successful, privately-owned company, OmniedRD plc ('OmniedRD'). This recruits, employs and manages teams of specialist and technical staff for overseas assignments under contracts with clients in the extractive industries. Its growth record and public profile makes it a particularly valued client at your office. At the end of the phone conversation in scenario 14, the client's accountant asks you about another, separate subject.

About five years ago, in accordance with its normal business, OmniedRD had recruited and supplied, on an extended contract to a client (a major mineral exploration group), a team of geologists and supporting staff. They had gone to work in a sub-Saharan country, known for its general corruption and chaotic bureaucracy. Two years after this team had started, OmniedRD had discovered (when organising another similar team for another, new client) that additional social security payments/state pension contributions now cumulatively estimated at £390,000 should have been paid to the provincial government. These were additional to agreed national taxes. Failure to realise that these were due had been a genuine oversight by both OmniedRD and, apparently, the provincial tax authorities. None of the individual expatriate contract staff for whom OmniedRD is responsible expect to derive any benefits from this province's social security/state pension arrangements.

OmniedRD had raised this matter with their existing client, the exploration major. There was general agreement that the extra monies were, legally, due and that under its contract these could be claimed by OmniedRD. Thereafter, the exploration major had started to pay monthly the additional monies to cover social security but had also, retrospectively, paid to OmniedRD its estimate of the outstanding £390,000 in full.

It had been formally agreed that this was to be a full and final settlement between the UK-based parties of the social security/state pension issue. The geologist team had been successful; its licence had been extended and the exploration major wanted a 'clean break' with as few complications as possible lest these jeopardise its relationships/ opportunities for further development in the region. The exploration major operates in fierce competition with several other multinationals that have far less scruples in their approaches to facilitating access.

With the additional monies agreed, OmniedRD had immediately started to pay the provincial social security contributions for all staff, on both contracts. However, it had not offered to do so retrospectively, nor had this been requested by the provincial tax authorities. Apparently, the increased sums had not drawn any attention to the past failure to comply. OmniedRD is therefore continuing to hold the £390,000 in its list of creditors.

OmniedRD's accountant repeats the explanation from last year. The provincial government has a history of creating unreasonable demands for other foreign operators, particularly those known as being susceptible to paying bribes. Currently, OmniedRD has good working relationships in the country, in part due to its past international approach of 'tough but fair' dealing. There is considerable fear that if the prospect of back-payments is raised unexpectedly, then, despite the voluntary nature of any admission, fines and demands for late interest payments far in excess of the £390,000 will very likely be levied. If OmniedRD attempts to argue or limit these, the on-going and future operations of both the exploration major and of the new client could be put in jeopardy. OmniedRD believes it is now (and has been for some time) in full compliance with local laws relating to all staff for which it is responsible. In respect of the past, 'sleeping dogs should be left to lie'.

Nevertheless, OmniedRD's directors recognise that a risk of claims could continue for some time. The period of entitlement to claim by the provincial government is unclear and initiating enquiries might rouse suspicions. They have explained to your auditor colleagues that they intend to leave the £390,000 in creditors for at least six years, to conform to the UK's Statute of Limitations. Only thereafter will they decide whether the liability may crystallise and, hence, possible future accounting treatments.

Last year, as part of routine reviews, HMRC questioned OmniedRD's list of creditors. The Inspector suggested that either OmniedRD should cease evading legitimate taxes due overseas by paying up, or obtain formal agreement from the provincial tax authorities that the monies need not be paid. If this evidence is not obtained, or unless the £390,000 is repaid to the exploration major, OmniedRD should take the sum into the current year's Profit and Loss.

OmniedRD's accountant informs you that there has been no change in the situation. The directors have no intention of raising the matter with the provincial authorities. Nor does senior management at the exploration major want the distraction of discussing the matter further - that is why sub-contractors are employed! If a claim were to be raised, OmniedRD would be prepared to settle the £390,000 and reasonable interest, arguing vigorously for that as the upper limit. The accountant accepts that, logically, provision for this interest ought to be made annually but concedes that, in reality, all parties to these hypothetical negotiations would probably be significantly influenced by the prospects, at the time, of further work for OmniedRD and for its clients in the province.

The directors want you - as part of your ongoing role as corporate tax adviser - to present the case to HMRC for keeping the £390,000 in creditors. They do not consider that they have behaved unethically. The issue is not one of deliberate tax evasion rather a robust approach to commercial realities where OmniedRD has a deserved reputation for maintaining its integrity in difficult circumstances. They understand that they are taking a commercial risk. For them the UK tax pressure is an unnecessary complication and, in their view, it is your task as their tax adviser to help them to address and be relieved of it.

What do you do now?

Scenario 15: Analysis

What are the readily-identifiable ethical issues for your decision?

For you personally

Should you accept the remit to argue on behalf of OmniedRD's directors to HMRC that the £390,000 ought to continue to be held in creditors?

What do you recommend to your audit colleagues regarding the treatment of the known underpayment of Social Security?

For the CA firm

How do you support partners and staff to explore openly the different ethical dilemmas, expectations and traditions for international operations of clients?

Who are the key parties who can influence, or will be affected by, your decision?

'You' ; the client's accountant; the other owner/directors; HMRC; the provincial tax authorities; the auditors in the UK; the exploration major.

What fundamental ethical principles for accountants are most applicable and is there an apparent conflict between them?

Integrity	*Can you accept the remit for arguing the case with HMRC for the deliberate withholding of information/payment from the provincial tax authorities?*
Objectivity	*How do you remain uninfluenced by the importance of this client to your office?* *While there has been full disclosure to HMRC, how do you judge whether it is valid to withhold information from tax authorities in another jurisdiction?*
Professional competence and due care	*Assumed, and that you are seeking to maintain professional standards.*
Confidentiality	*What are your responsibilities in discussing this with audit colleagues?*
Professional behaviour	*What are your obligations in arguing with HMRC for non-disclosure to the provincial tax authorities?*

Is there any further information (including legal obligations) or discussion that might be relevant?

The precise details of the laws in this situation do not alter the underlying ethical dilemma.

Is there a conflict between the 'Guardian' and 'Commercial' strands of an accountant's responsibilities?

The CA is being asked to be an advocate for a 'Commercial' solution as a pragmatic response to a legal problem. Within the 'Guardian' role this may give a conflict of interest with the duty to uphold the rule of law.

Based on the information available, is there scope for an imaginative solution?

None is obvious.

Are there any other comments?

The situation is similar to that in scenario 14 but here there has already been full disclosure of information to HMRC. In effect, OmniedRD is taking a complex reputational and financial risk in deferring a decision on whether/when to disclose to the provincial tax authorities the non-payment of the social security. While the accounting treatment of this risk can be covered by a pragmatic judgement of what constitutes a 'true and fair' view, this approach fits less readily with tax regulations.

Scenario 16: The unwelcome phone call

As a CA in sole practice you have a client in the bathroom and kitchen fitting business. He is an able salesman but far less interested in bookkeeping and detailed accounting. You know that he had been anxious ahead of a scheduled VAT inspection. You have just received a phone call from him.

Your client seemed very cheerful. He told you that the VAT inspection team had found only few and relatively minor errors and there had been rapid provisional agreement in the afternoon on how to settle these. Your client felt that this happy outcome was probably helped because, earlier in the visit, the inspector-in-charge had asked about a particular kitchen hob on display in the showroom, which your client had then offered to supply at a very significant discount.

The inspector-in-charge had agreed to this and said his daughter would be coming to collect and pay cash for it tomorrow.

This is the second instance within a couple of months that you have heard from a client of this inspector making such personal purchases while on inspection visits. You commented that while the sale and settlement may have been coincidental, arranging private transactions in this way is very far from usual and will be in breach of the inspector-in-charge's code of conduct. Your client responded that he was not fussed, simply pleased that the hassle of the inspection should be over for another few years. Moreover, he has made a sale, even if at an unusually low price. It is clear that your client is unwilling to report the matter lest this prompt a renewed and fuller inspection (which might find some more serious errors) or risk, as he sees it, antagonising VAT officials.

What do you do now?

Scenario 16: Analysis

What are the readily-identifiable ethical issues for your decision?

For you personally

While you have no formal evidence of a conscious conflict of interest by this inspector-in-charge, what has been described to you seems to be part of a pattern of misconduct. Would it be an appropriate breach of client confidentiality if you now report this matter to HMRC?

For the CA firm

As 'For you personally' - in that as a sole practitioner you are the firm. However, have you identified a respected source of independent advice with whom you can share your own exploration of the issues?

Who are the key parties who can influence, or will be affected by, your decision?

'You'; your client; the Inspector; HMRC.

What fundamental ethical principles for accountants are most applicable and is there an apparent conflict between them?

Integrity	*Should you accept your client's lower expectations of the standards for regulatory officials, or impose your own?*
Objectivity	*How do you deal with the risks of offending your client if you urge that he reports the matter, or do so yourself?*
Professional competence and due care	*Assumed.*
Confidentiality	*Can you/should you report this to the inspector-in-charge's superiors, if your client does not do so?*
Professional behaviour	*Do you have a duty to disclose in the wider public interest?*

Is there any further information (including legal obligations) or discussion that might be relevant?

The code of conduct for relevant officials.

Is there a conflict between the 'Guardian' and 'Commercial' strands of an accountant's responsibilities?

Disclosure without his permission could antagonise your client and be 'commercially' damaging to you. However, in a 'Guardian' capacity it is appropriate to protest and report indiscipline and breaches of trust being perpetrated by 'Guardians'.

Based on the information available, is there scope for an imaginative solution?

No.

Are there any other comments?

There is no evidence that this type of misconduct is common in the UK. However, this situation has some parallels with scenario 10 and obligations for 'policing' under the Foreign Corrupt Practices Act and scenario 21 on reporting suspicions of illegal activity in the wider public interest.

Scenario 17: How much do you tell the finance director?

You qualified as a CA but are now CEO of the South-West England regional office of a management consultancy practice. Your main work is to co-ordinate and lead inter-disciplinary teams with skills in design, production and marketing. Yet you retain an instinctive interest in financial matters and you regard understanding the financial implications of projects commissioned by clients for their businesses as an important part of your consultant's role.

In recent years your practice has undertaken several, locally-based assignments on manufacturing efficiency improvements for a medium-sized, quoted group that is head-quartered in London but active across the UK. Ostensibly, it operates through a number of divisions, as determined by the marketing needs of the civil engineering specialities of its core business. In practice, actual line-responsibility appears to involve a more complicated (if confusing) matrix that places significant control with four semi-autonomous regional directors. The authority of these directors is enhanced by their seats on the group's ten-person main board.

You have carefully cultivated a good working relationship with Ian, as the director with overall responsibility covering the South-West Region. Ian comes from an engineering background; has been with the group throughout his career; received very fast promotion and has an aura of someone not lightly to be crossed.

You were pleased, three weeks ago, to be asked by Ian to look, as a matter of urgency, at 'Project K'. Apparently, he had been surprised and much irritated to be told informally of the likely deferral of previously agreed delivery dates for the manufactured components on this sophisticated design-and-build contract. Project K comes within Ian's line-responsibility primarily because of the geographical location of the factory that makes the key components.

Once on site, your team had rapidly discovered a range of difficulties with Project K. These had started with fundamental design faults but these now appear to extend deep into the manufacturing processes. It was also clear that various contracts would be breached. Litigation is likely to follow. Within a week your team had produced a prioritised list of actions. Promptly, by phone, you had warned Ian that much time, effort and cost will be needed to correct the problems. Under conditions of strict confidentiality, the team had then begun working, with a selected group of the factory's senior staff, to establish a revised schedule to take Project K to completion.

Within a fortnight, at a face-to-face meeting, you gave Ian and the factory manager your 'ball-park' estimate that the delay will be a minimum of three months. Although not asked for detailed costings, you provided the projection that extra direct costs are likely to be £7 million to £10 million for re-design and re-tooling. This is before the probable claims for compensation. Neither Ian nor the factory manager disputed your estimates. While the manager was clearly agitated, Ian thanked you for your provisional reporting and seemed calmly focused on the need to find robust remedies. On Ian's instructions, now-written, your team has been working on a formal report to specify detailed recommendations. Whilst still incomplete, these appear certain not only to support your rough financial estimates but also to suggest that the three months may be overly optimistic, as allowing no room for contingencies.

You are aware from your general reading of the financial press that the group has a mixed profitability record and rumoured difficulties with its bankers. You assume that the situation with Project K is likely to be seriously detrimental to the group's financial position, although you and Ian have not explicitly discussed this.

You still have another week before the final version of the report is due to Ian, when you receive a surprise phone call from the group's London-based Finance Director (FD). After brief introductions, he says:

Ian told me there was no point in ringing you but I thought I would track you down nonetheless. We have a board meeting starting in fifteen minutes. I need to know a date when your report on Project K can be expected. It was just last night that Ian informed me that he had asked your consultancy to look at the situation. I appreciate you have only just started, so that there are no reliable estimates yet. But Ian mentioned that Project K could incur around £4 million to £5 million in extra costs, with income delayed by, perhaps six, maybe even eight weeks.

Ian has sent apologies for the board meeting - a family funeral, I think - but I want the rest of the directors at least to know outline timings. Hopefully, Ian is being ultra cautious but if something does turn out to be as wrong with Project K as those numbers suggest, the extra outlays and deferred income has implications for Group cashflows. The full board will need to start planning remedial action sooner rather than later. So when do you think your report will be ready?

What do you do now?

Scenario 17: Analysis

What are the readily identifiable ethical issues for your decision?

For you personally

How do you maintain your professional integrity - by responding only to the question asked rather than alerting the FD/Board to the full seriousness that Project K represents?

Who is your client when considering Confidentiality? - the Regional Director, or the Finance Director and Main board collectively?

Who are the key parties who can influence, or will be affected by, your decision?

'You'; Ian; the FD and Board. Indirectly, investors, prospective investors and other stakeholders in the Group.

What fundamental ethical principles for accountants are most applicable and is there an apparent conflict between them?

Integrity	*Do you feel obliged to correct Ian's apparently deliberate misleading of the FD without first discussing the request for information and the situation with Ian?*
Objectivity	*Does loyalty to Ian and the south-west region (your region) outweigh a wider and deeper duty to the board?*
Professional competence and due care	*Assumed.*
Confidentiality	*Where are the internal boundaries for confidentialities relating to a client?*
Professional behaviour	*From a consultancy perspective (as opposed to that of an auditor), this is predominantly an internal matter where you have no direct responsibility for results or publication issues. However, from the perspective of the board, your information could assist them significantly with the discharge of their duties.*

Is there any further information (including legal obligations) or discussion that might be relevant?

It would be interesting and helpful to know why Ian has not given a full picture to the FD. There are several possibilities. While unlikely, it could be that he has not understood the financial implication. Despite appearances, he may be in personal denial that there is a problem. He may be negotiating another job and he wants more time before Project K's problems are more widely known. However, these possible explanations are peripheral to the main fact that he has, apparently, wilfully misinformed the Group's FD and, by implication, will not want you to contradict him.

Is there a conflict between the 'Guardian' and 'Commercial' strands of an accountant's responsibilities?

'Commercially', you wish to remain on good terms with both Ian and the FD although, in terms of new work Ian, as the regional director, has been the primary focus of your previous attention. By contrast, your 'Guardian' role would persuade that you report fully and promptly what you know to the FD, even if with a disclaimer.

Based on the information available, is there scope for an imaginative solution?

Possibly, attempt to contact Ian to get his explanation/agreement to your contradicting him, but this is unlikely to be possible before the board meeting, given that he is attending a funeral.

Are there any other comments?

There are some, superficial, similarities with scenario 11, 'Interim results', where there is a problem of communications at client board level. However, in scenario 17 you are not an auditor. Nor is the problem concerned with the wider publication of financial information. Moreover, in this instance the internal client communication issues are about what seems wilfully incorrect, not inadequate, information. While your relationship is more detached, the situation is, possibly, more serious in that the future going concern of the Group could be under threat.

This is another instance where the circumstances for the CA are both lonely and with minimal time to think before your decision has to be implemented.

In your own reasonable interests, you may wish to ensure that your practice's fees for this consultancy work are settled promptly.

Scenario 18: Auditor or administrator?

It is Friday afternoon. You are an insolvency practitioner and specialist in corporate recovery with a CA firm that has a multi-disciplinary practice. A year ago, following a chance meeting, you were invited by a local entrepreneur to review and comment on the financial situation of his wholly-owned group of companies in the high-tech end of the construction industry. You diagnosed a classic case of 'over-trading' in a soft market, exacerbated by serious cash flow difficulties on three particularly large and difficult long-term contracts. For each of these contracts there are separate companies, albeit with the same directors for the holding company and each of the subsidiaries. There are some complicated cross-holdings between the companies.

You quickly set about recommending remedies and equally quickly the entrepreneur and his team implemented most of these. On many small contracts, outstanding debtors were substantially reduced. On the long-term contracts, you recommended better monitoring, reporting and billing arrangements. With these controls in place and continued market recovery, future prospects have looked much better. The entrepreneur and the group's bankers expressed their pleasure with progress.

With periodic visits, you built up a fair knowledge of the intricacies of the different contracts and developed a good working relationship with both the entrepreneur and the key directors and managers. It was very satisfying when your firm were asked to provide a quote for the group's audit and you have assisted your auditor partner in preparing and submitting an 'audit requirements' proposal. The entrepreneur told you this would be uncontested and that he has already told the existing auditor firm of the coming change. You knew that the proposal had been due for formal approval at a meeting of the holding company's board earlier in the week, on Wednesday. However, somewhat unexpectedly, neither your partner nor yourself received any contact.

A few minutes ago, the entrepreneur's very efficient PA (who is also the company secretary) has phoned you. By way of friendly introduction, she assured you that on Wednesday the directors had agreed to your firm's appointment as auditor for all the group companies. A letter on this will be in the post. But quickly she goes on to describe how almost all of the scheduled business of the meeting had been replaced by the breaking news of a potentially devastating crisis. This had been the warning of the unexpected and imminent financial collapse of the overseas-based customer for the two biggest contracts. For the last 48 hours, there has been intense discussions and re-working of projections while trying to get firm information.

With the dire situation confirmed this morning, the directors, on legal advice, have concluded that they have no alternative but the early appointment of an administrator at two of the group companies. Although far from certain, they hope that this can secure continuity as going concerns for the rest. The bank, as the biggest creditor, has suggested yourself, due to your familiarity with the complexities of the businesses and known ability to work with the key managers. At a meeting, just ended, the board were in complete agreement. As company secretary, she is now calling to obtain your agreement.

You respond to the PA/company secretary that the adminstratorship could cause you a conflict of interest with the audit appointment for the group. She replies that this was completed in a rush, without discussion, at the board meeting's end. However, as is her style, she had prepared the formal minutes (including the minute regarding the audit) directly after the meeting, as a first draft. She had also prepared letters notifying your firm and the previous auditors of the directors' decision. She has given these to the entrepreneur but knows he has not had time to look at, or sign, any of this documentation. She is quite happy both to get the letters back in order to destroy them and also to delete the minute about approval of the new auditors. She doubts that when the minutes go to the board for formal approval, any of the directors will notice, or if they do, raise the matter. They are now pre-occupied over the contracts and their own future careers.

What do you do now?

Scenario 18: Analysis

What are the readily-identifiable ethical issues for your decision?

For you personally

Does the directors' formal approval of the group audit appointment now prevent your appointment as administrator?

Do you have any conflict of interest through your past involvement or does your knowledge of the business give a greater benefit - as the bank and directors agree?

Because of technicalities, the audit appointment may be invalid (the other firm have not yet resigned and your firm has not yet accepted on behalf of subsidiaries). However, is it appropriate, to minimise doubt, that you accept the company secretary's offer to amend the draft minutes as a record of the meeting?

For the CA firm

How are partners and staff supported for making and reviewing such decisions?

Who are the key parties who can influence, or will be affected by, your decision?

'You'; the entrepreneur; the PA/company secretary; the directors; other prospective administrators; creditors.

What fundamental ethical principles for accountants are most applicable and is there an apparent conflict between them?

Integrity	*Can you accept alterations to the draft minutes of a formal meeting, to tidy up a technicality?*
Objectivity	*How do you draw the boundaries between the financial incentive to take on the administration role (rather than the perhaps very short appointment as auditor) and adherence to long-term standards that exclude the dual appointment?*
Professional competence and due care	*Assumed as high.*
Confidentiality	*What arrangement can you accept from the PA/directors that does not cause discredit to yourself and the profession?*
Professional behaviour	*Are the necessary rules for the prevention of potential conflicts of interest - between being auditor and being an administrator - being followed in spirit?*

Is there any further information (including legal obligations) or discussion that might be relevant?

No.

Is there a conflict between the 'Guardian' and 'Commercial' strands of an accountant's responsibilities?

While there seem to be sound 'Commercial' and pragmatic grounds for accepting the 'administration' in this instance, the detail of the regulations would normally exclude the partner of an auditor on the grounds of conflict of interests with the different demands of a quasi-'Guardian' role. Going ahead with accepting the administration may give the appearance of disregard for the legal/ethical requirements.

Based on the information available, is there scope for an imaginative solution?

No.

Are there any other comments?

No.

Scenario 19: Creating 'reservation of title'

You have just been appointed as receiver for a small food catering business and are at its ready-meals processing unit. From just a quick survey of the latest financial data it is clear that while profitable, its underlying funding is in serious disarray. You have made the decision that by continuing to operate the business for at least the coming week you can satisfy immediate customer needs without disruption. This will also keep the workforce together, and, hopefully, you will able to secure a quick sale to a trade buyer. Having prospective customers and established systems for supply and delivery should be worth a premium over the otherwise minimal knockdown value of the fixed assets. This should cover your fees, the preferential creditors and give something to the bank. However, unsecured creditors will be very unlikely to get anything by way of dividend.

You have spoken to the workforce. Now, in the office you take a phone call from a very anxious supplier. He has just heard of your appointment. He wants to return with a truck to collect the containers of deep-chilled, uncooked chicken that he had delivered yesterday. He has a number of unpaid invoices and he greatly regrets not getting cash when the goods and invoice were handed over yesterday. He claims he has retained 'title' and can link invoice details to specific batches of chicken by way of 'production' and 'use by' dates on the containers. Each container is clearly marked as sourced from his business. He therefore claims that the contents are still his.

Politely, you ask him to phone you back tomorrow as you have many pressing demands. Moreover, you need to check the situation. He asks for two minutes of your time. You agree. He stresses to you how urgent the matter is for him. He thinks he can find another buyer for the chicken meat but it is a perishable product. For good measure, he adds how critical doing this is for his business. Industry margins are very slim. He cannot afford to lose the cash flow involved. Although you know he is not going to admit to an insolvency practitioner just how tight his situation is, you get a real sense of fear in his voice that, in a chain effect, his business too could go under. After five minutes, you repeat your request that he phone back tomorrow. He says he is coming round anyway and will be with you in half-an-hour.

The processing unit's foreman, who is in the office, tells you the batches of chicken are in distinctive containers in the chilling rooms, still unpacked. Some of the contents will be needed for meals being prepared over the coming week but there is at least, he thinks, three week's supply if the containers are not moved out of the refrigeration area. The foreman offers to unpack the containers immediately and to scatter pepper on top of all of the chicken batches. He says:

> *That way you can tell him we have already started to process the chicken meat. We have done something of value so we have the title and he can't take the goods away. We can always hose off the pepper when we actually need to prepare the meals.*

Clearly wishing to be helpful, the foreman then adds:

> *But if the chicken does get taken away, we have spare deep-frozen duck breasts that would see us through a week. The customers would be happy. They'll be relieved to get anything. Duck as a substitute would be a classier dish.*

Time is short and you cannot start getting into detailed negotiations now. Being able to claim that the chicken has already been further processed should give you legally-defensible grounds for refusing to allow it to be taken away. Conversely, you could instruct that when the supplier arrives he be allowed to remove what he delivered yesterday.

What do you do now?

Scenario 19: Analysis

What are the readily-identifiable ethical issues for your decision?

For you personally

Whatever the precise letter of the law in relation to reservation of title, do you allow the anxious supplier to take back goods, which have clearly come from him and for which he will not otherwise be paid, or do you rely on an artificial process to refuse his request? This could be an acute situation for him - is that a factor that should influence you?

Do you see your key priority as concentrating on keeping the maximum flexibility to continue 'your' new business in order to find a buyer that will maintain it and its workforce?

Should you spend time and effort in trying to split the consignment so that the supplier can take away part - mindful that this compromise may open up a dispute over reservation of title on the whole?

Should you spend time and effort in trying to determine how realistic the foreman's suggestion is about the duck substitution for a week, so allowing the chicken consignment to be taken away?

For the CA firm

How are partners and staff supported for making and reviewing such decisions?

Who are the key parties who can influence, or will be affected by, your decision?

'You'; the supplier; the foreman (in offering advice on options); the workforce; the customers; the creditors.

What fundamental ethical principles for accountants are most applicable and is there an apparent conflict between them?

Integrity	*Do you act with integrity if you instruct the foreman to carry out a process solely so that it will create a legal justification for ignoring the claim to reservation of title?*
Objectivity	*Should you concentrate solely on the task for which you are appointed, hence doing what appears in the best interests in monetary terms for your new business responsibility (for bankers/secured creditors) - provided only that it is legally permitted?*
Professional competence and due care	*Technical ability and legal knowledge assumed.*
Confidentiality	*How can this supplier be treated with appropriate consideration while there are many urgent and competing demands?*
Professional behaviour	*How do you ensure that the insolvency processes are seen as being as fair as is possible, while suppliers retain their own responsibilities for choosing to whom they sell and for collecting their own payments?*

Is there any further information (including legal obligations) or discussion that might be relevant?

Assume that the scattering of pepper is a form of processing that would validly allow transfer of 'title' of the goods supplied.

Is there a conflict between the 'Guardian' and 'Commercial' strands of an accountant's responsibilities?

As the receiver you have a quasi-judicial role set up specifically to try to create the best commercial/working solution to a problem where society is most likely to benefit from the orderly re-arrangement of the business. Under significant time pressures and within legal constraints, you must evaluate between their competing claims, balancing both a 'Guardian' and a 'Commercial' role. While it is inevitable that some participants are likely to benefit more than others, the bankers involved in awarding future appointments are likely to be those who will monitor most closely the impact of your recurring decisions, and particularly your ability to make recoveries that benefit the banks as creditors.

Based on the information available, is there scope for an imaginative solution?

No, apart from instructing staff to explore the compromise of the duck substitution.

Are there any other comments?

No.

Scenario 20: Gazumping

Acting as an insolvency practitioner, 'you' had put up for sale a Glasgow property under the Scottish system of having a fixed closing date. Several offers were received and the best accepted. Lawyers for both parties are close to concluding the missives.

A third party, whose sealed bid had been unsuccessful, has now approached your manager with an unsolicited, revised offer that is very substantially more than the one accepted at the closing date. The increased consideration, if you accept this new offer, should more than cover the actual compensation that the original successful bidder can be expected to win in negotiations, even if, vociferously, he demands much more.

As your manager points out, it is in the interests of all the creditors, indeed of all the parties except one, that either you accept the new offer directly or you set a new round of bids and a second closing date. The only exception would be the original bidder who believes that he has had his offer successfully accepted but, as the manager points out, is about to get a real bargain.

Apparently, the original bids were all speculative by property developers. However, a supermarket has now expressed a serious interest and this has significantly increased the opportunity's potential and changed the risk projections.

You have discussed the unsolicited, revised offer with your legal advisers. They confirm that although there are likely to be protests, accusations of bad faith and a threat of legal action, halting the current process and having a new second round is a pragmatic possibility. Creditors should, thereby, make a significantly better recovery. This in turn should enhance your reputation among those most frequently instrumental in the award of insolvency appointments. Conversely, although undeservedly, you may in future become known as the person who sold off a valuable site very cheaply.

What do you do now?

Scenario 20: Analysis

What are the readily-identifiable ethical issues for your decision?

For you personally

Do you raise doubts as to the integrity of the established property bidding system in order to make a higher overall recovery on behalf of your 'clients' (effectively the bank and other creditors) and thereby enhance your reputation with them? Do you risk becoming known as the person who sold off a valuable site very cheaply?

For the CA firm

How are partners and staff supported for making and reviewing such decisions?

Who are the key parties who can influence, or will be affected, by your decision?

'You'; the previously successful bidder; the creditors; new prospective bidders.

What fundamental ethical principles for accountants are most applicable and is there an apparent conflict between them?

Integrity	*Would re-opening the bidding process be seen as being honest and fair by others?*
Objectivity	*How can you set aside the potential impact on your reputation in making your decision?*
Professional competence and due care	*Technical competence is assumed but would re-opening the bidding show superior commercial competence?*
Confidentiality	*Assumed.*
Professional behaviour	*Would re-opening the bidding discredit the profession generally and yourself in particular, with the original successful bidder, even though compensation is paid? Do you have a duty to support the existing procedures despite the enhanced benefit to the creditors?*

Is there any further information (including legal obligations) or discussion that might be relevant?

No. Assume the reliability of the legal advice that compensation would be lower than the new consideration.

Is there a conflict between the 'Guardian' and 'Commercial' strands of an accountant's responsibilities?

The 'Guardian' role would wish to support existing legal structures/ arrangements and the wider 'Commercial' world will tend also to endorse the sanctity of contracts for long-term relationships. However, as an insolvency practitioner, the banks are most likely to be your long term 'customers'. They (and the creditors) may support a 'robust commercialism' - getting a larger sum and paying compensation - as being in their interests, and so to your longer-term benefit.

Based on the information available, is there scope for an imaginative solution?

Discussion with the original bidder on an increased consideration to match that of the unsolicited offer might be an appropriate compromise. However, if it lacks transparency it may serve only to antagonise all parties.

Are there any other comments?

No.

Scenario 21: 'Dark 'n' stormy'

You are a taxation partner in an international firm. After meetings in the US you have stopped over for a long weekend on an idyllic island that is also a well-known centre for financial services. You are having a leisurely lunch in your small hotel reading a novel when a group of five, middle-aged to elderly men occupy a table near to your own. They seem to have been at a board meeting and are annoyingly determined to carry on in the dining room their earlier discussions. Without intending to listen, snatches of their conversation attract your attention.

They appear to be discussing awards and pricing for a variety of contracts for the provision of specialist healthcare equipment in the UK. Because you have a client in this industry, you recognise two of the company names being mentioned, despite these being relatively unknown to the general public. After lunch, you see that the hotel's small conference room has a notice reserving it for a meeting of 'EXJ (2001/2010) Reinsurance Company'. The name seems vaguely familiar.

That evening you are at the bar, sipping a 'Dark 'n' Stormy' rum cocktail. One of the lunchtime group arrives and you strike up a conversation. He explains that the other three visitors of his group have left for an evening round of golf being hosted by the fifth, locally-based member. Whilst initially guarded, with each 'Dark 'n' Stormy', your dining companion (as he has now become) turns progressively more garrulous. You discover that he has recently retired as a senior sales manager after 33 years with one company in the specialist healthcare equipment industry. He retains links to that company, having been appointed as a part-time, independent consultant, advising its Chief Executive Officer on pricing in competitive sales pitches.

You also discover that this is only his second visit to the island but he expects to be coming regularly, once a quarter. He has been appointed as the company's confidential representative to the board of an industry-specialist insurance company. Yet, he seems to know relatively little about insurance. Gradually, more details emerge and, putting these together with what you overheard at lunchtime, you conclude that the quarterly insurance meetings, as well as making some general decisions about insurance, may also provide a convenient front for the liaison meetings of a specialist industry cartel.

When, eventually, you are introduced to the other three, on their return to the hotel for a nightcap, you gain the clear impression that each has previously held a senior position in their respective, but rival, companies. Based on casual remarks, you sense each is still in a position to advise current management. You realise that by paying them, as directors of an offshore, captive insurance company (that requires genuine insurance premiums) the cartel/liaison/consultancy services could also be both discreetly facilitated and rewarded, without any explicit UK connections.

Your companions seem uninterested in your professional background. By contrast with your own, naturally curious, nature, they show no inclination to press you to reveal your professional links as adviser for a multinational group, one of whose subsidiaries had featured at the lunchtime discussions you had overheard and whose 'representative consultant' seems to be at this insurance/cartel meeting.

On your return to the UK, a short study of the relevant files confirms to you that this subsidiary does indeed contribute premiums to 'EXJ (2001/2010) Reinsurance Company' and has a small consultancy contract with one of the people whom you met briefly that evening. However, if not surprisingly, in neither the insurance documentation nor the official consultancy contract (copies of which you find in the files) is there any reference to quarterly liaison with competitors. Rather, prominent with the Group's published financial statements, is its 'Ethical Code'. This expressly prohibits any employee participating in illegal or improper activities and emphasises an approach of 'fair-dealing' with all stakeholders.

You are not familiar with the detail of the UK Competition Act but you know enough to realise that the observations and connections that you have made could be of interest to the Office of Fair Trading and to senior NHS procurement officials. Without further enquiries, you have no means of finding out whether or not the Group's main board are aware of these arrangements. Moreover, you are uncertain as to how much of what you know is through access to privileged information of a client and whether alerting the Group's main board could inadvertently constitute 'tipping off'.

What do you do now?

Scenario 21: Analysis

What are the readily-identifiable ethical issues for your decision?

For you personally

How do you balance the obligations (and distractions) of public duty with reasonable expectations for self-interest?

Clearly the least demanding approach is to do nothing - you only have suspicions; you have only developed these through chance and you have no direct duty to take this further. Does it matter that no one else will know if you choose to do nothing and say nothing?

However, unless ordinary individuals are willing to challenge corporate malpractice when found (if only by passing on information for others to investigate) then illegal activity is more likely to be perpetuated. Conversely, are you tempted to act as a 'whistleblower' out of a wish to display your 'cleverness'?

If you choose to inform your fellow partner(s) in audit, they may have more obligations. Although the client's main board/its most senior management may eventually appreciate your having prompted them into an investigation of their subsidiary (and through that exposure of the workings of the cartel) they may not - depending on how much their ethical code is for real, rather than for rhetoric. Should this be a factor for you?

For the CA firm

Assuming you have decided it is appropriate to pass on the suspicions/findings to an audit colleague, should there be further investigation/discussion with the client's main board - perhaps through its Audit Committee? Could this be deemed 'tipping off' and so should referral be made instead directly to the Office of Fair Trading (OFT), even though this may all be a product of a misunderstanding?

Who are the key parties who can influence, or will be affected by, your decision?

'You'; the directors of the subsidiary; the directors of the main board; OFT on behalf of the wider public; your fellow partners.

What fundamental ethical principles for accountants are most applicable and is there an apparent conflict between them?

Integrity	*Given the imponderables and that you may get little thanks for informing, should you over-ride the silence of self-interest?*
Objectivity	*What is the task in hand and your obligations to it?*
Professional competence and due care	*Assumed - however, is there a temptation to display your cleverness?*
Confidentiality	*Is your discovery in any way privileged through access to client information, but even if it is, are there waivers/ obligations for reporting directly to the OFT?*
Professional behaviour	*Having made this chance discovery, does an obligation of wider public service, which goes with being a professional, require you to follow it through - either through your own report, or with a fellow partner? How much should a duty of public service outweigh the inconvenience to yourself of reporting?*

Is there any further information (including legal obligations) or discussion that might be relevant?

More precise legal requirements of the Competition Act, although the apparent collusion among competitors appears contrary to fair dealing with customers.

The risk of appearing to 'tip off' may require that you obtain legal advice, even though this is a cost for which you (and your firm) are unlikely to be re-imbursed.

Is there a conflict between the 'Guardian' and 'Commercial' strands of an accountant's responsibilities?

There is a 'Commercial' risk for you and your firm in engaging with an aspect of a client's affairs that its main board may construe as beyond your remit and as unhelpful 'freelance' probing of areas that they see as confidential. Conversely the main board may be genuinely pleased to be able to take proactive steps to investigate their subsidiary's activities and, as necessary, to take timely action to avoid future reputational risks and penalties. In a 'Guardian' capacity, early recourse to a regulator such as the OFT with your suspicions would be the most appropriate.

Based on the information available, is there scope for an imaginative solution?

The 'compromise' route - that you discuss this with the Group engagement partner who then informs the Chair of the Group Audit committee - may run counter to the prohibitions against giving early warning to interested parties of potential regulatory investigation. While presupposing that you have made the personal decision that you ought to report your suspicions, how you do so may be a judgement call that needs to be made in conjunction with fellow partners. This in turn could be dependent on their advice as to whether the Group is serious over its approach to its ethical code.

Are there any other comments?

The temptation is to do nothing. But this may confirm the general adage, 'Bad things happen when good people do nothing'. There are some parallels in this scenario with the issues in scenarios 10 and 16.

Scenario 22: Quango interview panel

As a respected and established member of the regional business community, you have been asked to sit on the selection committee and interview panel for the competitive recruitment of a CEO for a publicly-funded/grant awarding enterprise body.

One of the applicants, Jack, is known to you from previous encounters. Principally, this was when he was operations director at a private sector business that was your firm's audit client. For some time you had thought his performance there to be weak, at times bordering on the unprofessional. This view had been hardened when, four years ago, your firm had been formally commissioned to investigate one aspect of his work. This had revealed a series of minor financial irregularities as well as deficiencies due to technical incompetence and lack of objectivity. Moreover, there were also unanswered questions as to his personal integrity in cleverly and knowingly covering up discrepancies over a number of years.

In that there was insufficient evidence that would sustain a criminal prosecution, disclosure of the findings had been properly limited to his employers. However, you were far from surprised that, shortly afterwards, Jack had moved to another job. It is from this that he is now applying.

The other interviewers all seemed impressed by his CV. This is supported by reports of his performance during earlier stages of the selection process, organised by independent recruitment agents, which make him the front-runner for the CEO post.

What do you do now?

Scenario 22: Analysis

What are the readily-identifiable ethical issues for your decision?

For you personally

How do you resolve expectations of 'confidentiality' in contrast with the 'public interest' element inherent in professional behaviour?

What is necessary for your own personal 'integrity' - should you declare, with minimal explanation, an interest and opt out? Or is opting out a 'cop out'?

How do you show 'objectivity' - do you remain fully involved and try to determine if the enhanced profile seen by other members/the recruitment agents may represent a genuine change or whether there is some flaw that, based on your own skill and judgement, you are able to identify without disclosing your grounds for prejudice?

You were asked to join the panel for your own competencies - is it fair on the other applicants, the prospective employer, or even the candidate if you do not give your full and frank assessment, plainly and openly?

Is there a temptation to take the approach that you are an unpaid volunteer; you are just one of several selectors; 'experts' are involved in the process and if Jack is selected as CEO and eventually repeats past errors, responsibility is widely divided?

Who are the key parties who can influence, or will be affected by, your decision?

'You'; Jack; fellow panellists; other applicants; the stakeholders of the publicly-funded body - including the general public.

What fundamental ethical principles for accountants are most applicable and is there an apparent conflict between them?

Integrity	*While you could ask to opt out of Jack's interview, does this deal fairly and truthfully with the issue and still allow you to play an appropriate part in the selection process?*
Objectivity	*How do you make an assessment of Jack's suitability for the CEO post that has full regard to ALL the considerations relevant to the task but no other?*
Professional competence and due care	*Assumed - as leading to your appointment to the selection committee. Would seeking to say nothing on the grounds of confidentiality be a misuse of the fundamental principle that requires due skill, diligence and care in the discharge of the duty?*
Confidentiality	*How do you respect the expectations of confidentiality from when you undertook the investigation and reconcile these with the other principles?*
Professional behaviour	*Do you have an over-riding duty to the community and society in that you were selected (even if unpaid) to assist in making an appropriate appointment and what would the general public's expectation be?*

Is there any further information (including legal obligations) or discussion that might be relevant?

No, unless there is specific guidance from the group that constitutes the funding body.

Is there a conflict between the 'Guardian' and 'Commercial' strands of an accountant's responsibilities?

No. While you are primarily in a 'Guardian' role and the CEO post has primarily a 'Commercial' dimension (so that empathy with its demands is an important aspect of your role as interviewer) both 'Commercial' and 'Guardian' roles value the 'capability' and 'competence' of leaders.

Based on the information available, is there scope for an imaginative solution?

Not obvious. You may wish to discuss this with the Committee's chair (or deputy if you are the chair). However, this may do little more than pass the ethical decision to someone else.

Are there any other comments?

No. The effectiveness of the selection process may be questionable but such imperfection is often an inevitable part of a subjective recruitment process.

Scenario 23: Recruitment and being a trustee

You are a trustee and member of the Governing Board of a not-for-profit organisation where you chair the recruitment sub-committee. This has the delegated power to offer posts on behalf of the Board. You have been advertising for a new Finance Director (FD) and have received a number of what seem strong applications.

One of these is from Henry, who is currently employed as Deputy Finance Director at another not-for-profit entity where the CEO is Sheila. Although Sheila is a fellow trustee and member of the Governing Board, she is not on the recruitment sub-committee. Hence, you decided not to tell her about Henry's application, fearing that this might give rise to a conflict of interest for her. Moreover, Henry had requested confidentiality, in terms of no contact being made to his current employer.

After the recruitment process has followed its scheduled course and concluded with interviews, the recruitment sub-committee have narrowly decided, on your casting vote, that the job should be offered to Henry rather than Angus. It was agreed that you should phone Henry next morning with the news about the impending offer. However, the recruitment sub-committee asked that, as a matter of both prudence and courtesy, you should first contact Sheila so that she is prepared in case Henry decides to consult her for more information before accepting the post.

When, this evening, you spoke with Sheila, her response, unexpectedly, was one of deep concern. She considers Henry to be very plausible and capable of impressing but, based on her own several years of experience of his work, to be incapable of taking on FD responsibilities and implementing commitments fully without strong and time-consuming support. While he gets on very well with the volunteers in the governance function, his full-time management colleagues find him feckless. She is pleased to know that he is seeking to leave his present post/her organisation. But she feels it is her duty to warn very firmly against making the offer on the grounds that he is likely to be a serious liability and long-term handicap for the existing senior staff at the not-for-profit where you are both trustees.

From past dealings with Sheila, you and the recruitment sub-committee members generally have a high respect for her judgement and personal integrity. The fresh perspectives she has provided mean that you now interpret some of Henry's responses to interview questions in a different, and less favourable, way.

You ended the phone call by saying that you will think further before contacting Henry. You now regret not having made this enquiry earlier but, at the time, it had seemed good practice not to do so.

You know that you yourself, at any time you wish, could choose to resign without notice from the Governing Board if relationships with the new FD go awry.

What do you do now?

Scenario 23: Analysis

What are the readily-identifiable ethical issues for your decision?

For you personally

Are you behaving with personal integrity in even considering that you could revise your casting vote on the basis of further information gained outwith the formal selection processes?

If you now recommend to the recruitment sub-committee that the offer be made to Angus, not Henry (and you do not also speak with Angus's employer) is the selection process being fair and objective, or unduly influenced by someone who was not at the interviews?

What is the impression that these changes will give to the other trustees/ management involved with the selection processes?

Should the best long-term interests of the Trust, its present management (and, perhaps, of Henry) over-ride any personal reservations that you may have over recommending to the sub-committee that they switch the offer to Angus?

How do you allow for the fact that you personally can withdraw from the governance functions of the organisation at any time - in a way that the paid employees cannot - if the new FD proves to be poor appointment?

Who are the key parties who can influence, or will be affected by, your decision?

'You'; the recruitment sub-committee members; Henry; Angus; Sheila and other stakeholders in the not-for-profit organisation.

What fundamental ethical principles for accountants are most applicable and is there an apparent conflict between them?

Integrity	*Should you proceed with the offer to Henry on the grounds that this was the fair result of an agreed process or recommend the alternative of Angus to the recruitment sub-committee as likely to be in the best interests of all parties?*
Objectivity	*How do you concentrate on the key consideration of getting the most appropriate person in post without being distracted by the requirements of other principles?*
Professional competence and due care	*Clearly, with hindsight, the process could have included more due enquiries beforehand, but should this remain a factor?*
Confidentiality	*Was the original intention of avoiding a conflict of interest (and so maintaining confidentiality at that stage) appropriate?*
Professional behaviour	*Do the apparent long-term interests of the organisation over-ride individual awkwardness at the change?*

Is there any further information (including legal obligations) or discussion that might be relevant?

It is assumed that all aspects of the recruitment process have complied with current employment legislation.

Details of the membership of the recruitment sub-committee - presumably a mixture of trustees and management - and their experience/competence for selection.

Is there a conflict between the 'Guardian' and 'Commercial' strands of an accountant's responsibilities?

No, there is both a 'Commercial' and a 'Guardian' interest in getting the most appropriate person for the post while maintaining the integrity of, and respect for, the pragmatic but imperfect systems of recruitment. However, a 'Guardian' trait may be to focus more on process than on outcome.

Based on the information available, is there scope for an imaginative solution?

No - unless a probationary period is included and carefully monitored in relation to Henry.

Are there any other comments?

Would the ethical situation be different if the decision to offer to Henry had been made by the recruitment sub-committee unanimously rather than on the basis of your casting vote?

Scenario 24: An alleged intimate relationship

You are the partner responsible for student training in a large office of a large firm. There is a clearly established policy, written into student contracts, that those who fail specified professional exams will have their training contracts terminated.

However, your predecessor introduced a discretionary arrangement of retaining some such students where there was 'good cause', because some very competent students sometimes failed, and also it was a pragmatic way to cope with periodic staff shortages. This arrangement is only loosely defined and you have discretion in making your decision, informed by a special, confidential report prepared by each student's senior manager, presenting factors for retention, or for termination.

The latest results season had ten failures. After gathering the reports and discussion with HR, you agreed that three students would be allowed to continue for a second attempt and that the other seven should be dismissed. This has been implemented.

One of the retained students is Yvonne. Supporting this decision, her audit senior manager, Philip, had submitted a seemingly well-balanced appraisal report. This was marked as being 'strictly private and confidential'. In her favour, he had explained that her failure could have been caused by her excessive diligence for the firm, with long hours spent on an unexpected investigative assignment for a client at a time critical to her studies. Moreover, it had also been noted that she gets on very well with clients and that staff members with her specialist interest (financial services auditing) are currently in particular short supply. However, he had acknowledged that her working papers were prone to technical errors and not infrequently lacked depth of analysis.

One of the dismissed students is Jim. His tax senior manager had been critical of his lack of commitment. At his exit interview, Jim, while reluctantly accepting the reasons for his own dismissal, had complained that the system of allowing 'good cause' to over-ride the termination clauses for selected students is unfair, and so unethical. As an example he cited Yvonne's case. He explained that he and she initially had worked together and they still enjoy a close friendship. He went on to say that Yvonne is currently having an affair with Philip, having previously had an intimate relationship with another manager with whom she remains on good terms.

Jim admitted that Yvonne had worked somewhat harder for the firm than himself. Nevertheless, in his view (and apparently also hers), her technical knowledge is weak but she has been consistently favoured in work allocations and assessments for reasons other than her competence, diligence or abilities as an accountant. Jim implied that there is a prevalent belief amongst junior staff that sexual liaisons can enhance career prospects - or, in Yvonne's case, help win a reprieve. He described widespread cynicism at the firm's claims that advancement is based objectively only on merit. As he succinctly put it, less 'true and fair', more, 'screw and all's fair'.

From Jim's convincingly accurate and detailed critique of what Philip had said in his supposedly confidential report on Yvonne and from your own (albeit limited) contact with her, Jim's allegations appear credible. You have re-read Philip's report. There is no reference or hint of the alleged relationship. You have confirmed the factual point that Yvonne did charge overtime during the investigation, although not nearly as much as Philip had implied. While you have no substantive evidence that the report has been unduly biased in her favour, you no longer trust its impartiality.

Philip is well regarded within the firm and is ambitious, having recently been put on the 'prospective partners' list. His wife trained with your firm and was a popular and respected manager. There was regret when she left, shortly after she married Philip, to work for a client. Three months ago you met her at a social function when she was heavily pregnant. Recently, during the planning phase for one of your client's audits, Philip took paternity leave following the birth of their son. You are likely to be working closely with Philip over the next few years and, in due course, will be asked to write a report on Philip's suitability to become a fellow partner.

What do you do now?

Scenario 24: Analysis

What are the readily-identifiable ethical issues for your decision?

There appear to be at least five issues, with each having progressively wider and more protracted implications. Distinctions between 'personal' and 'the firm' perspectives may be helpful for this analysis. However, repeatedly needing to distinguish between 'personal' and 'the firm' may indicate irreconcilable, longer-term tensions.

For you personally

Firstly, are you satisfied that it is it appropriate that the issue of Yvonne's retention (as relates to her as an individual) is now history; hence her next exam results will be the prime determinant as to whether she will continue to be employed by the firm?

Secondly, the principal and immediate challenge, therefore, becomes how you respond to the allegations from Jim in relation to Philip. How, discreetly and appropriately, do you investigate whether he had an undeclared conflict of interest when drafting the confidential report on Yvonne? Alternatively, do you ignore the allegation on the pragmatic basis that you cannot act in relation to Yvonne on the conclusion of any such enquiry? Do you then ignore the allegation on the grounds that the subject would be an awkward, possibly too much a private matter, to raise in any formal manner with Philip? Conversely, if you do not clarify (at least to your own satisfaction), what would be the possible implications of your unconfirmed suspicions for your future working relationship with Philip? Might your diminished trust impact on his prospects within the wider firm in ways that are, possibly, unfair? Should you give any consideration as to his personal/family circumstances, or are these irrelevant to the essential matter under consideration, namely whether his preparation of a report on Yvonne may have involved a conflict of interest that he should either have avoided arising, or subsequently disclosed when he was asked to write the sensitive appraisal report?

For the CA firm

The third, more long-term, issue is whether the discretionary element of the partial retention policy is fair. It seems to fit pragmatically with the needs of the firm and the continuation of competent students who have been 'unlucky', but may give the impression of, and occasion for, manipulation. However, is this, relatively, a minor manifestation of a bigger challenge?

The fourth, still broader, issue flows from Jim's implication was that this type of favouritism/possible exploitation is common within the office and causes consequent staff cynicism. This puts at risk morale and wider respect and trust within the firm. This could be exacerbated if there were to be recriminatory complaints and claims of abuse, harassment, or of unfair dismissal. However, can employers, legally or in practice, impose restrictions on relationships between consenting adults?

Fifthly, and generically, how can issues relating to personal relationships, often with sensitive implications, be faced among partners, senior staff and junior staff in a manner that is open, constructive and effective?

Who are the key parties who can influence, or will be affected by, your decision?

'You'; Jim; Philip; Yvonne; the firm's partners and staff at every level.

What fundamental ethical principles for accountants are most applicable and is there an apparent conflict between them?

Integrity	*Do you ignore Jim's allegations as being incidental to your belief that the firm's flexibility on its choice of students for retention, overall, operates a fair system? Do you need to establish whether unresolved conflicts of interest are undermining the credibility for impartiality (save for merit) of the firm - either specifically or generally?*
Objectivity	*How do you address any personal views on Philip's alleged extra-marital relationship to raise constructive discussion of the issues involved?*
Professional competence and due care	*Assumed - although you may need to discuss the arrangements with HR. Inadequacies in supervision and appraisal could jeopardise technical and professional standards if biased assessments of staff go unchallenged.*
Confidentiality	*How do you respect confidentialities while seeking to ascertain whether or not Philip's assessment has breached expectations of disclosed conflicts of interest?*
Professional behaviour	*It is essentially an internal matter for the employing firm, and individual CAs within it, as to how employment and promotion is conducted. However, respect and trust in firms for being quite consciously meritocracies is part of wider respect and trust in the profession.*

Is there any further information (including legal obligations) or discussion that might be relevant?

It is assumed that the dismissal/retention policy is legally valid.

This situation has firm-wide implications and a partner responsible for training is unlikely to operate in isolation. However, a CA needs to be alert to wider perceptions of the ethical environment wherever individual responsibilities lie.

Is there a conflict between the 'Guardian' and 'Commercial' strands of an accountant's responsibilities?

Staff retention and promotion policies that are widely accepted as fair are in the combined interests of both aspects of the accountant's role.

Based on the information available, is there scope for an imaginative solution?

Not immediately. However, wider acknowledgement of the significant complexities arising in such circumstances may point to longer-term solutions.

Are there any other comments?

There may be a further confidentiality issue, as to how Jim, presumably through Philip having shown it to Yvonne, knew the detailed contents of the confidential report recommending her retention.

Scenario 25: A fellow partner's alcohol problem

You are an insolvency partner in a medium-sized office of a medium-sized national firm. You have a good working relationship with your senior insolvency colleague, Peter, who is widely respected for his confidence, incisiveness and being exceptionally hard working. His appointments bring to the practice a very substantial fee income. This is most useful for the office, as your firm's centralised national executive makes increasingly strident demands for efficiencies and cutbacks in partners and staff.

However, you have realised that over the last few months Peter has shown increasing signs of serious stress. He had always been crisp, but previously he was careful to be courteous. Now, he seems to have adopted a bullying or snapping style of speaking with the firm's staff. Before, at new appointments, he emphasised that he was there to rescue and save jobs. Now, he seems to relish a reputation for wholesale redundancies and to use this to be unreasonably demanding and sneering with continuing staff. Once good-humoured and willing to explain, now he more often seems curt, morose and tetchy. Formerly only a social drinker, he shows a new tendency to consume larger amounts of alcohol, and not just at corporate hospitality events where his appearance of cheerful conviviality helps him to maintain useful contacts. On several occasions recently, you think he has appeared slightly unstable during the daytime.

Tentatively, you mentioned to Peter both the drinking and the staff vulnerability to his reactions. He brusquely dismissed them as figments of your imagination. You have discussed them briefly with two other partners. Neither offered any practical advice. You have therefore now raised the subject with Harry, the office's long-standing managing partner, albeit due to retire shortly.

Harry too has not welcomed the sharing of your concerns. He responded that Peter has had a particularly heavy workload of late. This has produced exceptionally high billings, which is good in that it should keep the firm's national executive quiet for another quarter. If Peter has been gruff with some staff or had a few extra drinks to help tide him through stressful jobs, then fellow partners should be grateful. Certainly, they should not seek to cause embarrassment through championing staff's complaints or pestering Peter about personal habits.

Moreover, Harry has hinted, not very subtly, that in his view your comments are driven either by jealousy of Peter or, and more likely, by an attempt to position yourself as his, Harry's, successor as managing partner. He tells you that the welfare of partners and staff is his concern, not yours. You do not need to adopt a managerial role. It is presumptuous to criticise another partner's style - particularly that of a star biller, such as Peter. Rather, the best practical way for you to help Peter and the office is to stop gossiping, to do more work in your speciality and get more billings yourself. From now on, Harry does not want you to raise again the subject of Peter's drinking habit with him, with other partners or with Peter.

It is true that if offered Harry's post on his retirement - no successor has been designated and none are immediately obvious - you would accept enthusiastically.

What do you do now?

Scenario 25: Analysis

What are the readily-identifiable ethical issues for your decision?

For you personally

Do you have an ethical responsibility to raise concerns for the personal well being of another partner i.e. to challenge Peter's irascibility and drinking - in a professional situation where short and medium term monetary returns are the initiating purpose of the relationship? If so, how?

How do you work constructively within a system where an apparently-remote, central executive monitors and drives a practice driven through billings and where local senior management is reluctant to recognise the toll that there might be on partners and staff?

How do you ensure that your own self-awareness recognises the extent to which your response to Harry may be influenced by some combination of:

- *your personal ambition;*
- *your recognition of the longer-term benefits of Peter retaining his competence;* or
- *genuine concerns for a colleague, the firm's staff and clients' staff?*

For the CA firm

How can supportive working relationships be developed and maintained so that individuals are respected as 'ends' rather than merely 'means', while recognising the competitive environment in which services are provided for fees?

Who are the key parties who can influence, or will be affected by, your decision?

'You'; Peter; Harry; other partners; firm's and client staff.

What fundamental ethical principles for accountants are most applicable and is there an apparent conflict between them?

Integrity	*How do you respond to your realisation of Peter's apparent emerging alcohol addiction in a way that could be most effective for the holistic interests of Peter, others and yourself?*
Objectivity	*To what extent can you isolate your personal interest in becoming managing partner with concern for Peter's health and style?*
Professional competence and due care	*Assumed at a technical level, although inadequacies in support could jeopardise technical and professional standards.*
Confidentiality	*How do you balance more effectiveness through openness against discretion/confidentiality in discharging any responsibility you may have to help Peter conduct himself in performing his professional work?*
Professional behaviour	*Is there an ethical issue if you disobey the explicit instructions of Harry and raise the subject of Peter's condition with Peter or with other partners?* *Such situations may arise in any workplace. Although this is essentially an internal matter for the partnership, it has wider long-term implications for the profession as to relationships between members.* *Honesty with courtesy to others, even if hard to specify, is an attribute of professional behaviour.*

Is there any further information (including legal obligations) or discussion that might be relevant?

There could be health and safety implications if excessive pressures are placed on Peter but this is a more complex area than the scenario allows.

Is there a conflict between the 'Guardian' and 'Commercial' strands of an accountant's responsibilities?

The role of an insolvency practitioner has different relationships from that, say, of auditor or tax adviser, being more akin to that of a state appointed 'Guardian' than that required of a more 'commercially-focused', client relationship. A more authoritarian or arbitrary style may be possible (and necessary) than where the client can discontinue the relationship - hence there may be less immediate commercial need to rein in the results of Peter's excesses with his daily contacts (except those who can influence appointments). Conversely, as agents, insolvency practitioners are more overtly active in commercial transactions than auditors or tax practitioners.

Based on the information available, is there scope for an imaginative solution?

You may take the view that the most ethical approach is to leave the matter as instructed and hope to be appointed to the managing partner role where you may be able to deploy a more focused approach to supporting Peter. However, delay may be injurious to Peter.

Are there any other comments?

Although this is largely a systemic problem - of workloads, billing pressures and channelling personal ambitions - the issues have an individual ethical dimension and consequences for individuals.

Scenario 26: Reasonable encouragement or devious deception?

You are a middle-aged tax partner in a medium-sized national firm based in a medium-sized city. You have productive and friendly working relationship with Jane, who has been with the firm since qualification and who, on your recommendation, has recently been appointed senior manager in your specialist area. Jane is, in your view, both technically very competent and justifiably popular with clients and staff. She seems set to complement your own client service very successfully and significantly enhance your part of the practice.

You also know that Jane has a strong ambition to become a partner. Although you have never previously discussed it with her explicitly, you believe that this is the prime motivator for her having stayed with the firm and for her working long hours to ensure the notably profitable management of her client portfolio (within your overall supervision). However, from confidential discussions with your fellow local partners you know that there is very strong support for another candidate with another tax speciality to become a partner in about 18 months' time. You fear that this appointment would almost certainly be fatal to Jane's prospects as you doubt your ability to make the business case that both should become tax partners in this office. For reasons connected with their families' circumstances, it is very unlikely that either candidate could readily relocate.

Should Jane decide to leave now, you have little doubt that she could gain a senior manager post with another firm in the city and could, in due course, achieve partnership there. Not only would this represent potential future competition; meanwhile, you would severely miss her potential contribution to sustaining and growing your own practice area. It would be hard to find a replacement who is both as keen and as able.

You have been undertaking staff appraisals all day. Jane's is coming up next. After the congratulations are over, she is very likely to ask you for frank guidance - 'a true and fair view' - as to her career prospects with the firm.

What do you do now?

Scenario 26: Analysis

What are the readily-identifiable ethical issues for your decision?

For you personally

Whether or not she asks, do you offer Jane a frank assessment of her prospects and of the potential difficulties of making a business case (within the boundaries of confidentiality reasonably to be expected by your fellow partners and the circumstances of other employed staff)?

Or, do you give this only if Jane asks you directly?

Or, if Jane asks, do you give her an evasive answer?

Or, do you positively encourage her with the prospect that a partnership will always be possible if she continues to work for you/your firm, thus leaving her to discover for herself that an offer of partnership (such as she can take up) is unlikely to be forthcoming?

In short, how much ethical responsibility do you have for advising openly on another person's career where you have an obvious vested interest in the decision?

For the CA firm

How can supportive working relationships be developed and maintained so that individuals are respected as 'ends' rather than merely 'means', while recognising the competitive environment for employment and promotions?

Who are the key parties who can influence, or will be affected by, your decision?

'You'; Jane, and her family

What fundamental ethical principles for accountants are most applicable and is there an apparent conflict between them?

Integrity	*Trust within your working relationship with Jane will be very important to provide a professional service to clients but can there be a reasonable boundary whereby career prospects within pragmatic employer/employee relationships are not discussed?*
Objectivity	*Can you provide a frank assessment of Jane's prospects when your own - but probably divergent - financial interests are closely bound up with hers?*
Professional competence and due care	*Assumed.*
Confidentiality	*Does the confidential nature of internal assessments of other candidates and of future business allow you to claim this as an area that is 'off limits' for discussion, or, more controversially, where you can give knowingly misleading answers?*
Professional behaviour	*Complexities over employment and promotion are not confined to the accountancy profession. However, the development of collegial trust within a profession requires fostering.*

Is there any further information (including legal obligations) or discussion that might be relevant?

No.

Is there a conflict between the 'Guardian' and 'Commercial' strands of an accountant's responsibilities?

The 'Guardian' role, which would normally have a more hierarchical structure than that of a 'Commercial' entity, might have reduced expectations of transparency. It might therefore appear more acceptable to 'deceive' Jane as to her prospects for the sake of the task and expect her loyalty in understanding this. Moreover, ambiguity of prospects may be seen as part of a necessary, healthy and stimulating competition within the delivery of professional services, as currently structured, in that it encourages individual performance. However, this may seem disloyal to a respected colleague. From a 'Commercial' perspective, collaboration and respecting voluntary agreements are to be promoted.

Based on the information available, is there scope for an imaginative solution?

You may be able to stress the training and related benefits that your firm can offer while acknowledging that no specific promises can be given. It may be a fair part of Jane's overall reward package that she has the incentive to push herself and to learn from this, even though you may know that her prospects are more limited than she realises, for reasons unrelated to her personal performance. However, through her persevering, events may prove otherwise.

Are there any other comments?

Is the 'conflict of interest' that you face so obvious that it can only be for Jane to make her own assessment of risks and decisions, provided that you do not deliberately mislead her?

Scenario 27: A personal reference

You are the Director of the Finance Service at a 'not-for-profit' social business. Five years ago you made the personal decision to resign from a more lucrative professional post in order to 'make a difference in society' as you see it. Aspiring to improve standards, you have worked hard to introduce tighter internal systems and to enhance inter-departmental relationships. Along the way, this has helped mould the accounting/finance staff into a more effective and dedicated department, happier both together within the team and with employees and volunteers elsewhere in the organisation.

Then, two years ago, you recruited a new deputy, David, who, while technically competent, has increasingly sapped your own job satisfaction. You also sense it has been debilitating within the Finance Service. Broadly, some of your longer-serving staff members have commented informally to you that they find it irritating how David often seems unwilling to share information without being pressed. Some volunteers have also told you that his attitude to them has made them consider resigning. However, as far as you are aware, none have formally said this, nor have any actually left. More specifically, there is a serious tension between yourself and David. He seems to resent any suggestions that you offer and to be incapable of coping with even mild criticism without taking offence. He has several times stated that he feels he is being unfairly harassed and bullied when you consider that you are simply requiring 'best practice'.

You have discussed this situation informally, with the CEO. While she has found David sometimes awkward and defensive, and she knows that the Director of Care Services considers him unnecessarily abrasive, she has not herself encountered any specific problem that would warrant disciplinary action.

An uneasy gloom has diminished your enjoyment of work and you know that David has commented to others how stressful he finds working with you. Then, after one particularly frosty fortnight, David informed you that he had reached the shortlist for Deputy Director of Finance at another social business of a similar size and structure to your own. He believes that he will be a strong candidate at the final interviews in a fortnight's time. Quietly, you feel elated at the prospect that he might be leaving.

Next day, that feeling evaporates when you receive a letter from the CEO of David's prospective new employer. Typically, David had put your name down as his referee without having first asked your agreement. The practice at your organisation is that each Head of Service who acts as line manager should respond to requests for references for staff in their section. Hence, you now need to provide a written reference and answer a questionnaire ahead of the final interviews. Questions cover the ability of the candidate to work in teams, to motivate volunteers and to accept advice. Your honest answers to these can only be negative.

For several reasons - organisational and personal (for him and for you) - you would very much like David to get this other post. However, you are also proud of your principles and that you seek to uphold integrity and objectivity, for yourself, your profession, your organisation and for the 'not-for-profit' sector.

What do you do now?

Scenario 27: Analysis

What are the readily-identifiable ethical issues for your decision?

For you personally

How do you manage the conflict of interest of wanting to give a positive reference to encourage David's successful appointment - and thus removal of a distraction from your own work - while discharging your sense of integrity and public service obligations that would give a more critical assessment?

Who are the key parties who can influence, or will be affected by, your decision?

'You'; possibly your CEO; David; staff at the other organisation; staff at your own organisation.

What fundamental ethical principles for accountants are most applicable and is there an apparent conflict between them?

Integrity	*How do you give advice that is truthful and uncorrupted by self-interest?*
Objectivity	*How do you achieve a state of mind that has regard to all the considerations relevant to the task in hand but no other?*
Professional competence and due care	*Assumed.*
Confidentiality	*Assumed.*
Professional behaviour	*How do you discharge fairly your obligations to the third parties that rely on references?*

Is there any further information (including legal obligations) or discussion that might be relevant?

While there are legal cases concerned with the giving of employment references and of managing relationships with colleagues that may influence the detail of responding to this situation, the broad issues have an ethical dimension that remain.

Is there a conflict between the 'Guardian' and 'Commercial' strands of an accountant's responsibilities?

The 'Guardian' instinct may be to give a franker assessment. The 'Commercial' instinct - even at a not-for-profit business - may look for a solution that seeks to remove the barriers that you see as inhibiting your work and that of the other members of the finance team (including David's).

Based on the information available, is there scope for an imaginative solution?

In that this problem has been raised in the past with the CEO, it may be preferable either that she completes the reference or independently reviews a draft. Alternatively, you may choose simply to write a reference of your composition and not complete the questionnaire.

Are there any other comments?

Although a very well-known dilemma affecting many professional/commercial situations - hence double meaning phrases such as 'you will be lucky to get this person to work for you' or 'this person should go far' - the giving of references recurred as a challenging and confusing area for CAs to uphold their ethical values.

Scenario 28: How much should money matter?

Just under six months ago you joined an accountancy firm that has for some years been successfully developing a speciality in providing a range of financial and tax advisory services to medical practices across a wide geographical area. One of the firm's partners, who is approaching retirement, has devoted significant time and effort in giving you training; in sharing methodologies; in developing your own expertise; and is introducing you not just to existing clients but to prospective ones also. At the three-month stage you were offered in writing an equity partnership, starting nine months thereafter, six months from now. Orally, you accepted.

Earlier today you received an unsolicited personal approach by a 'head-hunting' employment agency acting for a larger, rival firm and inviting you to an informal interview. It is seeking to develop in the same field and the prospective terms being quoted offer you equity partnership, which would start also in six months time. Over the years, it is likely to give larger partnership distributions. Nothing in your present contract could be enforced to prevent your acceptance of this new offer, although you know it would seriously disappoint your current employers (both the retiring partner and your intended prospective partners), were you to accept it.

You sense that they will feel that they have trusted and relied on you, so that if you do transfer to the other firm you will be letting them down. Their clients too may think that there is a loss of continuity but when you raised this as a reservation with the head-hunter, she intimated that this should not inconvenience them as you would be expected to encourage as many as possible to transfer with you.

What do you do now?

Scenario 28: Analysis

What are the readily-identifiable ethical issues for your decision?

For you personally

Should an area as personal as your career options be bound by professional ethics - even though there are no enforceable legal constraints - if there is an economically more attractive offer unexpectedly available?

For the CA firm

How can the balance be found for a training firm between trusting and avoiding being open to exploitation?

Who are the key parties who can influence, or will be affected by, your decision?

'You'; your current employers (both the retiring and prospective partners); the rival firm; clients and prospective clients.

What fundamental ethical principles for accountants are most applicable and is there an apparent conflict between them?

Integrity	*Is it matter of integrity that, having given your oral agreement, you should stay with it despite the probable loss of long and short-term financial benefits?*
Objectivity	*How will you evaluate the differing claims of professional ethical considerations given the very personal nature of the choice?*
Professional competence and due care	*Assumed.*
Confidentiality	*If you move, will you use the detailed knowledge (including about clients and prospective clients) to the explicit advantage of your new employers/prospective partnership and disadvantage of your current employers/prospective partnership?*
Professional behaviour	*Whilst this may appear a more personal/intra professional matter than a public matter, clients from outside the CA profession may be affected. There may be a wider perception that you are breaching trust (even if unspecified) for personal financial benefits.*

Is there any further information (including legal obligations) or discussion that might be relevant?

There may often be some contractual restrictions in such situations but in that these are likely to be geographically limited, temporary and difficult to enforce, the importance of ethical considerations will remain.

Is there a conflict between the 'Guardian' and 'Commercial' strands of an accountant's responsibilities?

Respecting the demands of loyalty over the financial may be more a 'Guardian' virtue whereas it may seem 'commercially' appropriate that there be fluidity and flexibility in all employment arrangements, as stimulating competition and enterprise.

Based on the information available, is there scope for an imaginative solution?

Discussion with current employers (both the retiring partner and intended prospective partners) would mean that you could share your deliberations and explore the possibilities before making final decisions. In this way, any decision to follow up on the unsolicited approach; to attempt to negotiate new terms; or to leave (if that is your final decision) may be better understood.

Are there any other comments?

Would the ethical considerations and response be different if, either,

- *you had approached the employment agency? or*
- *you were already a partner?*

5 CONCLUSIONS

Paradoxically, this section is primarily concerned with what has been omitted from the report thus far. In part, this is because the reactions, conclusions and wider implications drawn by the readers in thinking or discussing the scenarios are of more practical significance than the musings of the researcher. In part too, it acknowledges the injunction of Epicurus, as cited on page 2 of the introduction, that ethics must concern itself with proceeding on from theoretical discourse to grapple with implementation. That can only happen in actions, not words. This section will therefore seek only to draw out what might be points arising from the scenarios that can contribute to ethical conduct.

The essential, but unstated, principle, of 'ethical courage'

An unstated but recurring theme of the scenarios is that 'ethical courage' must be a constant. Yet 'courage' is not stipulated in the ICAS Codes of Ethics.[1] Perhaps this seems understandable because, as noted in the Introduction, the popular image of accountancy-related activity does not evoke immediate images of bravery, boldness or stubborn heroism in the face of some traditional enemy. A reference to 'courage' might seem pretentious, even somewhat ludicrous.

Moreover, the distinction of 'ethical courage' is important. Lord Moran in his study, *The Anatomy of Courage*, which drew on his extensive personal observations during both world wars of persons of every rank (from private to Prime Minister), defined 'fear' as 'the response of the instinct of self-preservation to danger' (Moran 1945, p.19). 'Courage' is the 'will-power' to cope with that instinctive reaction. Deep apprehension is caused by the potential to lose something valued or loved. In some such circumstances, psychological courage or physical courage may be called upon. But 'ethical' or 'moral' courage is when the action needed to face up to unpleasant consequences is of itself ethically-charged.

Ethical courage is not something that can be developed readily within the relatively short scenario narratives or analyses, focused as they are in uncertain futures. Courage cannot be grasped by intellect alone or readily measured. More broadly, instances of sustained courage often cannot be described in public in that these would need the full detail of what had actually happened. Disclosure of 'courageous' determination (perhaps in refusing to concede to a client's demands), must be masked by respecting the rights of that same client to 'confidentiality'. A tightly-worded letter of resignation may be the only clue as to an honourable and painful defiance, with Beattie *et al.* (2001) offering a rare glimpse of the frequent struggles behind closed doors. Thus, the essential role of courage may become evident only by default. Hence, without having been able to highlight ethical courage directly in a scenario, it is necessary now to draw on a well-known example of where it failed on a systemic scale.

Whatever the exact detail from extensive subsequent analyses, the broad scenario can be portrayed succinctly as follows. Andersen, before its collapse in 2002, had received from several of its, now notorious, former clients consultancy income that was well in excess of audit earnings. The response to the firm's internal pressure on engagement partners and staff to secure these income streams was to devise for their client managements 'creative accounting' solutions. These were not necessarily illegal but exploited every technical loophole. Clever Andersen personnel were very skilled at finding these. Taken to excess, form and appearance prevailed over the substance of the underlying transactions. Tragically, too few of the firm's leaders showed the strength of underlying purpose, the 'ethical courage', to challenge the cumulative abuses lest the firm lose not just the audits but the whole engagements, and with it their own income and prestige. The public interest was subordinated to personal benefit.

The absence of courage at Andersen is an ethical issue because, as Barbara Toffler, a former 'ethics consultancy' partner in the US firm of Andersen, revealed in 2003, there was a lack of influential insiders prepared to take the risk of personal loss by challenging effectively an organisational culture where fear and greed had undue influence. Seemingly, key personnel preferred to conceal rather than insist on letting the truth prevail, even though 'seeking truth' and transparency are central tenets of accounting. For accountants, 'ethical courage' must be a key component in exercising proper professional scepticism, to challenge others both internally and externally.

It is instructive to note how and why Andersen's powerful and respected global network disappeared so quickly and comprehensively. This was especially surprising given the context that financial regulators, worried by the tight circle of an existing oligopoly, might well have sought its preservation. But financial regulators were pre-empted. Quite suddenly, while previously respected as distinctive and dynamic, Andersen was seen as soiled and untrustworthy. The actual catalyst was not sophisticated and was understandable to non-specialists: the judicial conviction of the firm, at its Houston office, for shredding papers required for an investigation. That shredding appeared to have been a response of self-preservation to danger which those involved lacked the ethical courage to resist.

Collectively, multiple decision-makers in the 'audit markets' decided the firm had been 'at the scene of too many accidents'. Fearing contamination by association, the leaders of the global 'Commercial' communities did not wait for the regulators, the legal guardians of the 'Guardians' to act, but rushed to replace Andersen with other firms themselves. The guardian US Supreme Court subsequently judged the verdict on shredding the papers to have been based on a mistrial, but this came far too late to save Andersen's reputation. A reputation for 'being ethical', had been already shredded, along with the paperwork.

Simply, Andersen's reported actions had breached public, commercial expectations of what should constitute ethical conduct.

Which ethical principles had been breached may seem, now, irrelevant. It was not diligence and technical competence - arguably the firm had tried too hard at these. From Toffler's account it appears that, intellectually, the need for the appearances of objectivity and integrity were well appreciated.[2] The firm had even sold 'ethical consultancy' as a service. What was lacking was 'ethical courage' to link the actuality of jeopardised principles to aspirational claims to excellence (that must inherently include ethics). Tellingly, Toffler (2003, pp 253-4) concludes by quoting from the 1947 funeral eulogy for Arthur Andersen:

> *Mr Andersen had great courage. Few are the men who have as much faith in the right as he, and fewer still are those with the courage to live up to their faith as he did.... Those principles upon which his business was built and with which it is synonymous must be preserved. His name must never be associated with any program or action that is not the highest and best. I am sure he would rather the doors be closed than that it should continue to exist on principles other than those he established... Your opportunity is tremendous; your responsibility is great.*

The will-power and energy for courage - to resist fears or excessive exploitation of professional opportunity for self-benefit rather than public service - is an ethical requirement that is hard to illustrate in 'what do you do now?' type scenarios. Many factors, of circumstances, of age and of position, may reasonably alter where, within a spectrum between timidity and temerity, the ethical answer should fit. But without ethical courage, statements of ethical principles may be very interesting academic ideas that serve little purpose beyond posturing. As such, if not then implemented, they may set standards that serve for indictment of professionals as hypocrites, who have done no better than covered self-interest under a veneer of piety.

Loneliness, agencies for professional support and the ethical essentials of 'conscience' and 'self-discipline'

One of the most striking remarks made in the research interviews was that of a former partner of a major firm. It was of the sense of 'loneliness' when making decisions with an ethical dimension. Perhaps, this might be because, as some of the scenarios illustrate, often a decision needs to be made swiftly, even instinctively. However, other circumstances may offer the luxury - or pain - of days or weeks for weighing up the options when there is no excuse for ignoring the duty to share with other partners or colleagues. Perceived isolation may be exacerbated by knowing the scale or size of responsibilities and risks and so a wish of not wanting to burden others. There may be some, often misplaced, sense of shame at having encountered the problem, or of bravery, that the difficult decisions need to be toughed out alone.

ICAS provides confidential support in these types of circumstances. By contacting either Member or Legal Services, a member (or person with valid links to a member) can seek guidance and an opportunity to explore the issues with an understanding and independent specialist. Similarly, many firms have their own arrangements for networks of advisers.

Although an attitude that seeks such support on encountering an ethical challenge - rather than having a sense of guilt, such as having caught some infectious disease that must not be passed on - is important, ultimately any ethical decision can only be personal. Hence each scenario ends with asking, 'what do you do now?' Interviewees emphasised the importance of a sense of personal conscience as part of the processes of ethical decision-making. It is noteworthy that the importance of 'conscience' for individual decision-making is of such importance that its freedom is expressly embodied in Article 18 of the Universal Declaration of Human Rights.

However, 'conscience', a major dimension to ethics, along with faith and religious traditions, remains beyond the scope of this report, save to make three observations. Firstly, the root meaning of the word 'religion' - 'a binding together' - is powerfully suggestive both of individuals serving a wider, public interest, and of doing so in community with others.

Secondly, following the insights of Goodpaster (2007), who has written specifically on the theme of corporate conscience and culture, it is an essential that a common dialogue and language develops between practitioners and educators in business and professional ethics. The former, who are daily formulating and implementing policies that have significant effects on the lives of many people, including their own, are the architects of conscience in corporate culture. The latter, through their own training in the methods and history of ethical reasoning, can act as the builders of common structures and conduits for constructive exchanges between present and future audiences. What is needed is that both architects and builders share a common language and literature. Scenarios that are accessible to both audiences seem the neutral and non-judgemental foundation for this.

Thirdly, 'conscience' is linked with 'self-discipline', the ability to control and restrain personal and professional power. This may mean that just because an opportunity has been identified it does not have to be exploited for short term gain. This may seem unfocussed, like weakness, for those ruthlessly intent on personal self-advancement, but accountancy's essential goal of 'balance' requires constraints and a principled concern for compromise.

If the language of 'conscience', of an understanding of 'self-control' and of 'balance' is not shared by colleagues - many possibly from other professional backgrounds or cultures - 'self-discipline' may indeed be a lonely pursuit. The existence of these anonymised scenarios, by enabling anticipation of potential problems and collective discussion of ethical issues, may enhance mutual comprehension of ethical positions.

Reflections on the 'Guardian' and 'Commercial' theme and the ethical principle of 'discernment'

As noted in the introduction, within the analysis for each scenario the question was posed, is there a conflict between the 'Guardian' and 'Commercial' strands of an accountant's responsibilities? Within the scenarios, the more frequent answer is 'yes' with the exceptions arising primarily in those that focused on more generic issues of people management or recruitment procedures. In these there is a common cause. 'Guardian' and 'Commercial' enterprise alike seek to retain or select staff on the basis of capability and competence.

Unfortunately, posing this question does not directly solve the problems. Rather it may help focus attention for accountants as to what, strategically, they are trying to achieve. It may then clarify what are the key tactical requirements for the role in which they are then involved.

In the ICAS (2006, p3) report, *Principles Not Rules: A Question of Judgement*, there is reference to the Diamond of Trust. This may be summarised as:

> *Responsible enforcement of accounting standards requires regulators to be willing to accept a range of judgement-based outcomes. Regulators need to be able to trust preparers and auditors, who in turn must be capable of exercising judgement.*

This diamond provides four points of referral between standard setters, auditors, regulators and other users and preparers.

Key concepts are those of 'Judgement' and 'Trust'. So too, these apply to professional ethics, although a triangle will suffice. Between the three reference points of 'Accountant', 'Guardianship' and 'Commerce', there needs to be trust as to the exercise of judgement such that the trust of each is not damaged, but rather is enhanced by individuals' or firms' decisions in addressing ethical dilemmas.

This triangle need not always be equilateral, with the different angles at times being more acute, with a tendency to caution, to prudence, such that the 'Guardian' interests may prevail. However, in every case there should be a conscious exercise of choice, balancing expectations but recognising that the privileged role of an accountant within society demands shrewdness of discernment and fulfilment of obligations.

Shrewd and discerning accountants will be willing to discuss and test their own judgements with counter-parties from different traditions or approaches, explaining the concerns and ethical reasoning and being open to alternative outlooks. 'Shrewdness' may not seem a natural phrase for ethical codes, suggestive as it is of some inscrutability, even subterfuge. Yet 'discernment' and 'worldly wisdom', exercised through careful calculation and balance, seem essential to best manage the inherent contradictions of the symbiosis of ethical instincts drawn from 'Guardian' and 'Commercial' traditions. 'Trust' must be a part of a 'Guardianship' that is instinctively less inclined to trust, and 'Judgement' part of a 'Commerce' that prefers flexibility and negotiated compromise. In essence, accountancy 'wisdom' is the confidence to apply personal competence through the exercise of personal integrity for a client and the broader public interest in an objective yet discerning way.

It remains an enduring human interest as to how to achieve such discernment. One means that has recurred in discourse about ethics, from at least the time of Aristotle, is through training. Most recently, Moberg (2007) charts a series of propositions for the progression of practical wisdom that begins with an openness to value not just experience but reflection and inspiration to give the capacity for wisdom-related performance. To achieve this needs also ethical imagination, a creative yet systematic mode of enquiry and the ability to re-frame ethical issues in a way that becomes intuitive, much as when a master player at chess has moved beyond the game's conventions. Beneficial outcomes are not confined to making personally-appropriate ethical decisions but, if accompanied by skilful communication, quality advice-giving, mentoring and dispute resolution may flow from it.

As a pre-requisite for the individual seeking wisdom there will need to be components of knowledge, of thinking and of emotional and motivational dispositions that are enhanced by social interaction and do not decline with age. The collective challenge for any profession, whatever is its syndrome, history or the nature of its competencies, will be to create situations where these components can be recognised, fostered and respected so that 'discernment in action' becomes an intrinsic feature of its members.

Wider reflections and the prospective role of accountants for the promotion of professional ethics

The medium of a research report is an appropriate opportunity for exploring professional ethics. It offers more scope to recognise the fullness of the range of complexities that come with messy reality than shorter journal papers allow, yet it benefits from a critical review by both practitioners and academics. It need not be structured, like a textbook, to specific lessons. A research report can be relatively succinct but avoid over-simplification, coupling both discipline-specific and cross-disciplinary insights with pragmatic guidance for the future.

In this case the positioning, as fifth in a series where the predecessors had established literature-based foundations, has enabled the drawing together of evidence and the posing of some questions. Mostly these have been looking at tactical applications of ethical thinking rather than grappling with a strategic vision. Yet, beyond the scenarios there is an important opportunity to probe the comfort zone of the accountancy profession by asking whether, an Institute or profession should consciously set out to promote higher standards of ethical expectation, and to provide ethical leadership to the society in which its members live.

Or, is it acceptable only to adopt and adapt to norms of contemporary 'best practice', while being under no obligation to try to transcend or enhance this?

As noted in chapter three, accountants, through the pervasive nature of their discipline that enters every aspect of society, have collectively a possibly-unique opportunity to influence standards of ethical conduct across an exceptionally broad range of activities.

For many busy accountants this may seem a challenge too far. They are not opposed to ethics but nor do they wish to be heroes. And yet they would be annoyed to be described as 'unethical'. They have trained for several years and subsequently worked hard to remain technically up-to-date, fulfilling duties with competence and diligence. They respect confidences and seek to be self-disciplined and objective. But, for the ambitious, the opinions of clients or bosses cannot be ignored. The summit of daily aspirations may be to balance the varied conflicts of interests encountered (of several other parties and not just of themselves) without giving too many hostages to fortune (or litigation). Being a professional has to be consistent with the recurring need to generate fee-income or earn a salary. This requires a combination of technical expertise, empathy and probity, not independent thought alone. Unlike for, say, a salaried academic with tenure, there may be no guaranteed income without clients. Careful calculation rather than courage may seem more compatible with paying the mortgage.

Such an approach, if less than an ideal, represents the apparent pragmatic necessity of getting on with a job within a system that is based on a compromise, but is still working. The temptation to consign the Andersen debacle to a 'one-off' (caused by excessive greed and rule-based thinking by distant individuals) is not necessarily complacency. Searching for a vision of a different utopia may seem a luxury for which the resources of time, space or energy appear unaffordable.

This report, like its four predecessors, tries to persuade otherwise and it seems greatly to ICAS's credit that it should fund and facilitate these studies. The collective willingness of ICAS to do so represents already a risky 'taking-to-heart', even an act of heroism, that might counter the negativity cited at the end of chapter three.

As with the absence of model answers, this report may be lacking in that yet again it does not specifically answer the questions it has just posed. The justification is this. Only practitioners, of and for themselves, can decide on their willingness to be proactive in such a role. Regulators might nudge or overtly encourage. Some in society might scorn any bid to shape a wider ethical culture. To attempt a leadership role might appear arrogant for a profession with what some might suggest has a parasitic relationship with entrepreneurial business, as society's primary economic generator. But expressed as part of the symbiotic relationship of 'Guardian' and 'Commerce', it suggests both an opportunity and a responsibility for leadership.

To be proactive requires widespread consensus, following broad agreement among the members who bear the significant and direct personal costs of participation. However, if implemented, this would be accountants drawing on their twin foundations within the 'Guardian' and 'Commercial' traditions to play a leadership role within society. It would also require ethical courage, discernment and self-control.

Although a report, even a series, can only prompt such thoughts, not deliver answers, hopefully the contribution of the series can come in informing the detailed debate. It is up to the present and emerging generations of accountants to determine the roles and routine functions of accounting within society, and thence what ethical attributes must be delivered in practice. For accountants in the UK that debate is developing. As this report has moved to its final stages, ICAS (2007) has published its 'Clearly Ahead' Strategy that highlights integrity, wisdom, innovation and service, whilst ICAEW (2007) has launched the initiative of 'Reporting with Integrity' seeking widespread consultation on what this core ethical attribute means, especially in the context of providing information for better markets.

So, with professional ethics, a profound, enduring, and yet changing challenge is that each individual within each generation needs, at least periodically and perhaps even continuously, to keep exploring issues of ethics, each for themselves. The benefits of all this exploring are not just for themselves but must also become apparent in widespread public use across the multiple activities that accountants straddle. Hopefully, too, along the way, practitioners and other interested readers can enjoy, or at least find stimulating, rising to the potential challenges of ethics in addressing the questions of 'What do you do now?'

Endnotes

1. 'Ethical courage' is recognised in IEPS 1 (IAESB, 2007). Para 48 states: '*Professional accountants and students develop ethical courage as they observe the decisions of others made in accordance with the fundamental principles of the Code of Ethics. IFAC member bodies can work with employers, mentors and others to highlight examples of ethical courage, and bring this to the attention of students and professional accountants during pre- and post-qualification accounting education programs*'.

2. Even had Andersen followed the aphorism '*Honesty is the best policy*', this might have failed in the longer term. Bishop Richard Whatley (1854), in his Apothegms, noted that '*he who is governed by that maxim is not an honest man*'. For where there is a deliberately and overtly calculating approach to relationships there can never be a sense of deep trust or certainty. One party may always fear being caught out by the other's unsignalled decision to switch to 'dishonesty', as suddenly that becomes the best policy. It is noteworthy that the root Latin word 'honestas' meant simultaneously both 'ethical excellence' and 'reputation'. There could be no hollowing out. For a public person in an intimate society, the latter was impossible to achieve without the former.

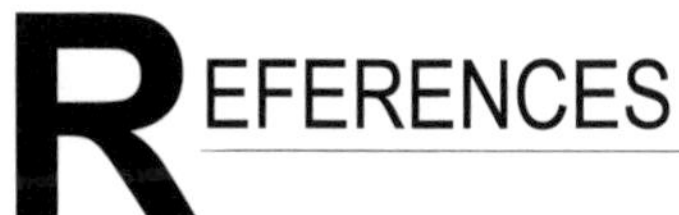

REFERENCES

As noted in the introduction, this report has sought to avoid duplication of bibliographic material that can be found in the three literature reviews covering *Ethics in Business, the Individual Professional Accountant* and *the Professional Accounting Firm*, which have been previously published in this series.

Literary and older sources

Aristotle, *The Nicomachean Ethics* (trans. Thomson, J A K, 1953) Penguin, Harmondsworth.

Elliot, T S (1944), *The Four Quartets: Little Gidding,* Faber, London.

Epicurus, *To Marcella 31, Text 124,* in Inwood, B & Gerson, L P (1994) *The Epicurus Reader,* Hackett, Indianapolis.

Homer *The Iliad* (trans. Rieu, E.V., 1966) Penguin, Harmondsworth.

Moran, Lord (1945), *The Anatomy of Courage*, Constable, London.

Plato, *The Republic* (trans. Lee, H P D, 1955) Penguin, Harmondsworth.

Rowling, J K (1997), *Harry Potter and the Philosopher's Stone,* Bloomsbury, London.

Rowling, J K (2007), *Harry Potter and the Deathly Hallows,* Bloomsbury, London.

Sophocles, *Antigone* (trans. Watling, E F, 1947), Penguin, Harmondsworth.

Whatley, R (1854), *Apothegms*, cited in Partington, A (ed. 1992), Oxford Dictionary of Quotations, Oxford University Press, Oxford.

Professional and academic contemporary sources

Beattie, V A, Brandt, R & Fearnley, S (2001), *Behind Closed Doors: What Company Audit is Really About,* Palgrave, Basingstoke.

Cheetham, G & Chivers, G (2005), *Professions, Competence and Informal Learning,* Edward Elgar, Cheltenham.

Goodpaster, K E (2007), *Conscience and Corporate Culture,* Blackwell, Oxford.

IAESB (International Accounting Education Standards Board) (2007), *IEPS 1: Approaches to Developing and Maintaining Professional Values, Ethics, and Attitudes,* International Federation of Accountants, New York.

ICAEW (Institute of Chartered Accountants of England & Wales) (2004), 'Additional Guidance on Ethical Matters for Members in Business', *Accountancy Magazine,* September, pp 132-141.

ICAEW (2007), *Reporting with Integrity,* Institute of Chartered Accountants of England & Wales, London.

ICAS (Institute of Chartered Accountants of Scotland) (1854), *Royal Charter* cited, Chambers, R J (1995), *An Accounting Thesaurus: 500 years of Accounting,* Pergamon.

ICAS (2004), *Taking Ethics to Heart* (Eds. Helliar, C & Bebbington, J), A Discussion Document by the Research Committee of The Institute of Chartered Accountants of Scotland, Edinburgh.

ICAS (2006), *Principles Not Rules: A Question of Judgement,* Institute of Chartered Accountants of Scotland, Edinburgh.

ICAS (2007), *Clearly Ahead,* Institute of Chartered Accountants of Scotland, Edinburgh.

Jacobs, J (1992), *Systems of Survival: A Dialogue on the Moral Foundations of Commerce and Politics,* Hodder & Stoughton, Sevenoaks.

Llewellyn, S (1999), 'Narratives in accounting and management research', *Accounting, Auditing and Accountability Journal,* Vol 11 No 2 pp 220-236.

Lovell, A (2005), *Ethics in Business: a Literature Review,* Institute of Chartered Accountants of Scotland, Edinburgh.

Maclagan, P (2003), 'Varieties of moral issue and dilemma: a framework for the analysis of case material in Business Ethics education', *Journal of Business Ethics.* Vol 48 pp 21-32.

McPhail, K J (2006), *Ethics and the Individual Professional Accountant: a Literature Review,* Institute of Chartered Accountants of Scotland, Edinburgh.

Megone, C (2002), in Megone C & Robinson, S J, *Case Histories in Business Ethics*, Routledge, London.

Moberg, D J (2007), 'Practical Wisdom and Business Ethics', *Business Ethics Quarterly,* July Vol 17 No 3 pp 535-561.

Molyneaux, D, (2003), 'Blessed are the meek for they shall inherit the Earth - an aspiration applicable to business?', *Journal of Business Ethics,* Vol 48 pp 347-363.

Molyneaux, D C, Webster, L & Kennedy, D (2004), 'Scenarios in banking ethics: responses, reflections and commentary', *Business Ethics: a European Review,* Vol 13 No: 4 pp 255 -268.

Pierce, A (2007), *Ethics and the Professional Accounting Firm: a Literature Review,* Institute of Chartered Accountants of Scotland, Edinburgh.

Porter, M E (2006), 'On the Importance of Case Research', *Case Research Journal,* Vol 26 Issue 1 Winter 2006 pp 1-3.

Securities & Investment Institute (2007), *Integrity at Work in Financial Services,* Securities & Investment Institute, London.

Toffler (2003), *Final Accounting: Ambition, Greed and the Fall of Arthur Andersen*, Broadway Books, New York.

Yin, R K (2003), *Case Study Research,* Third Edition, Sage, Thousand Oaks.

Codes of Ethics

International Federation of Accountants (IFAC)
http://www.ifac.org/Ethics/Pronouncements.php

Institute of Chartered Accountants of Scotland (ICAS)
http://www.icas.org.uk/site/cms/contentviewarticle.asp?article=4830

United Kingdom, Auditing Practices Board (APB)
http://frc.org.uk/apb/publications/ethical.cfm